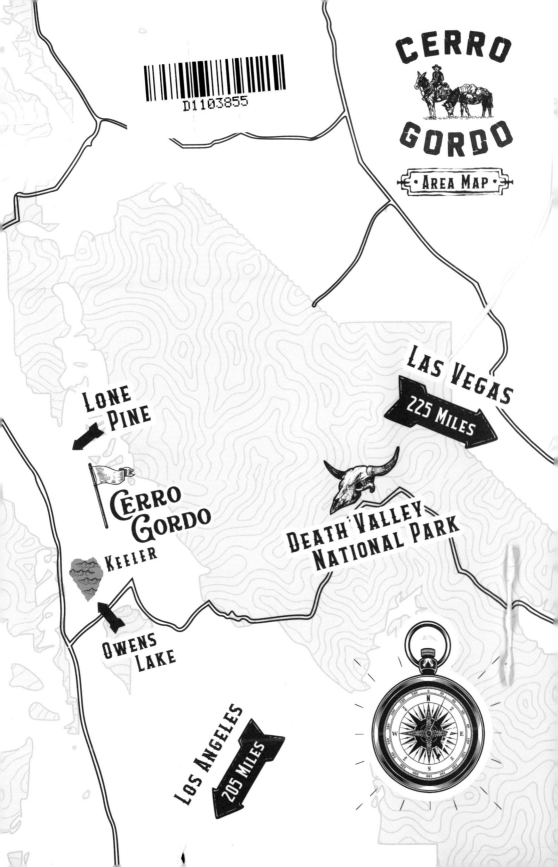

GHOST TOWN
LIVING

CERRO GORDO

EL. 8250

PRINCIPAL ORE DEPOSITS
OF UNION MINE

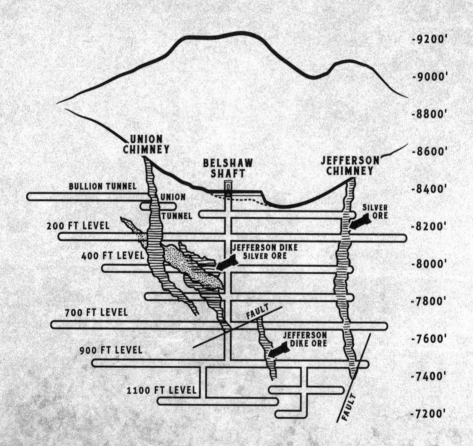

GHOST TOWN LIVING

MINING FOR PURPOSE AND CHASING DREAMS AT THE EDGE OF DEATH VALLEY

BRENT UNDERWOOD

HARMONY

NEW YORK

Published in the United States by Harmony Books, an imprint of
Random House, a division of Penguin Random House LLC, New York.
harmonybooks.com

Harmony Books is a registered trademark, and the Circle colophon is a
trademark of Penguin Random House LLC.

Library of Congress Cataloging-in-Publication Data
Names: Underwood, Brent, author.
Title: Ghost town living : mining for purpose and chasing dreams at the edge
    of death valley / Brent Underwood.
Identifiers: LCCN 2023021380 (print) | LCCN 2023021381 (ebook) |
    ISBN 9780593578445 (hardcover) | ISBN 9780593578452 (ebook)
Subjects: LCSH: Underwood, Brent. | Ghost towns—California—Cerro
    Gordo. | Cerro Gordo (Calif.)—History. | LCGFT: Autobiographies.
Classification: LCC F869.C444 U63 2023 (print) | LCC F869.C444 (ebook) |
    DDC 979.487—dc23/eng/20230817
LC record available at https://lccn.loc.gov/2023021380
LC ebook record available at https://lccn.loc.gov/2023021381

ISBN 978-0-593-57844-5
Ebook ISBN 978-0-593-57845-2
Signed edition ISBN 978-0-593-79814-0

Printed in the United States of America

Book design by Andrea Lau
Jacket design by Pete Garceau
Illustrations by Rebecca Noel Ati
Front-jacket photograph by Arnaud Montagard
Back-jacket photograph: Courtesy of the author
Author photograph: Courtesy of the author

10 9 8 7 6 5 4 3 2 1

First Edition

For my parents, Liz and Bill, and my sister Laura

CONTENTS

FIRE

AIR

PREFACE

I am the age of most of the ghosts that live here.

The men and women came from all over the world.

Sailing ships from China.

Fleeing the famines in Ireland.

Farmhands and cowboys.

The tenements of New York City.

Small towns across the Midwest.

They came here to make their fortunes, in search of adventure . . .

. . . and most of them died. Died before age thirty-five.

They died of exposure. They died in famous mine collapses. They died of influenza and diseases they picked up in the brothel here. They breathed in lead dust in the Union Mine and got sucked into machinery. They died in gunfights over card games. They died of suicide and alcoholism and little cuts that got infected. Some are buried in the cemetery here, some are still trapped down in the mines.

They worked twelve-hour days and seven-day weeks for subsistence-level wages. They had dreams of enormous riches, of escaping the strife of their homeland, of a different kind of life. They died of heartbreak and homesickness and were buried below wooden headstones now lost to time. The sardine cans they subsisted on and discarded, the Prince Albert tins they tucked claim papers in—it's this evidence that I find in washes and in gullies that testifies that any of them ever existed at all.

Not that this place was any kinder to the owners of the mines.

I am now the latest in the long line of owners, and nearly every single one of them was ruined. They made fortunes then lost them. They lost marriages and reputations. Their ambition curdles inside them, turning their hearts to stone. The only evidence that they ever existed is etched in the legal record of hundreds of now-forgotten court cases, newspaper scandals, and the occasional street sign. Obelisks mark their grave sites back in civilization. Only one chose to be buried here.

This town I am in, Cerro Gordo, is the rock of paradoxes.

To me, it is beautiful, but it is also dark. It is totally barren, yet it teems with the potential of life and natural wonders. It is a dreamscape that also holds the stuff of nightmares, a place built inherently on extraction that somehow manages to take a piece out of everyone who mines it. Something you think you own until it ends up owning you.

I am the luckiest man in the world. I am also a prisoner of this place.

I live at eight thousand feet, with one of the most breathtaking views in the continental United States. I see the highest peak and the lowest valley. Beneath me are mines so valuable they built the city of Los Angeles, mineral veins tapped for hundreds of millions of dollars' worth of silver, yet I am hopelessly in debt. I can sleep in my choice of a dozen ramshackle buildings, every one of them a piece of living history, a monument to the single-minded determination of the men who built them in this cruel, hard place . . . and yet nowhere can I reliably take a shower or brush my teeth.

It's a whole town that's mine, once home to some four thousand people and now has a population of me, myself, and I.

Dodge City. Tombstone. Deadwood. Virginia City. Bisbee.

Cerro Gordo started earlier and lasted longer, and yet, hardly anyone had ever heard of it. When it went up for sale in 2018, it cost me every single penny I had . . . but was still cheaper than a half-decent two bedroom house today in the city that probably wouldn't exist without it, Los Angeles.

It was my life savings, and every single day it has cost more. It is the best money I have ever spent. The best thing I will ever do. On some days, it feels like the last thing I will ever do.

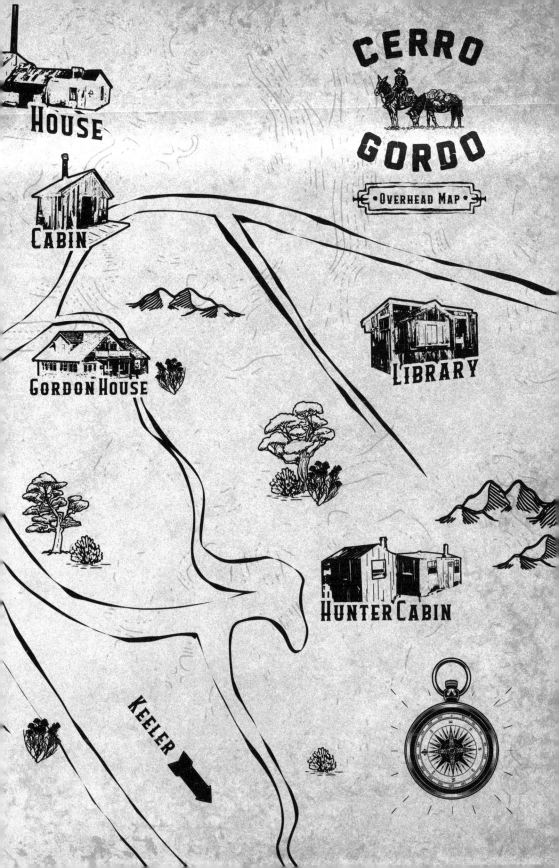

GHOST TOWN
LIVING

EARTH

If it can't be grown, it has to be mined. It's a truth of human progress. There is a monument to it out my bedroom window. A mountain of tailings—the jagged shards of broken stone hauled up from what was once the most prosperous silver mine in California and then discarded—looms over the town. When I stand atop it, I can see ore the miners rejected because it wasn't rich enough for them to process. Not good enough to refine into bars of pure precious metal.

Out beyond this mountain, beyond this man-made heap of rock that perches upon it, is the barren dust basin of what was once the great Owens Lake. Now a monument of a different type, the lake was drained to allow the city of Los Angeles to thrive. Beyond that, on the other side of the valley, there is the Sierra Nevada, lush with trees and streams. My cabin likely began its life across this valley. As part of those forests. That's where the wood was harvested to build the town of Cerro Gordo.

The forests don't go forever. Eventually they stop. As the trees approach the summit of Mt. Whitney, the air gets too thin for them. The soil, less fertile. One of those trees is the highest tree in the continental United States. Does it know that, or just that it's alone up there?

People didn't come to this side of the valley to grow things. They came here to mine. Billions of years ago, asteroids collided, dust stuck together, and the Earth formed. Molten lava pushed silver, lead, and zinc up to fill in the cracks in the contorting crust of the new Earth, nature's version of kintsugi, the ancient Japanese art of restoring broken things with precious metals, making them sturdier and more beautiful than they ever were before. A few billion years later, miners got word of the dead star debris here in the Inyo Mountains and flocked to set up camp and extract their little piece of it. Some found much, much larger pieces than others.

It's easy to think of Earth and the earth as separate things when you live in the city. You're so far removed from the source of anything created in the earth, that Earth itself seems more like an idea than anything else. That's what happens when you don't touch soil and you can't see starlight. They become novelties or abstractions. And that's when you forget that you came from the earth, too, along with everything you touch, and you will return there one day.

It's impossible to avoid these thoughts here. This town was established because of the earth around it. It's famous because of it. It's the reason I'm here. It's the reason I'm writing this. It's the reason you're reading this. It connects all of us. No matter how far removed from it we may feel.

Being here makes me feel more connected to Earth. And in turn more connected to everything in the earth, whether it be grown or mined.

CHAPTER 1

PICK YOUR SPOT AND SWING

It started as a pretty straightforward task.

William "Burro" Schmidt, a prospector, was tired of bringing his gold ore around a mountain, so he decided to go through it. In the spring of 1900, in the El Paso Mountains of the Mojave Desert, Schmidt began to chip away every day at solid granite using a pick, a shovel, and a four-pound hammer. When enough broken rock accumulated by his feet, he'd carry it out, first on his back in a canvas sack, and later in a wheelbarrow.

He'd come to the desert of California to save his life. Six of his siblings had died of tuberculosis back home in Rhode Island. Doctors, in their primitive ways then, had prescribed a hotter climate to avoid the same fate. Never one for half measures, Schmidt picked the hottest, driest desert in all of North America to stake his claim.

He reimagined himself as a prospector, a frugal one at that. He reinforced the toes of his boots with discarded tin cans and patched his tattered, greasy trousers with old flour sacks.

If you visit the tunnel, as I have, you begin to get a sense of the man, the compromises he was willing to make, and the ones he refused to. The first thing you notice about Schmidt's tunnel is that the farther back you walk, the lower the ceilings become. At 6'2" I stand comfortably at the beginning of the tunnel. A few hundred yards in, I have to bend down to avoid hitting my head on the jagged, dust-covered rock all around me. I wondered if Schmidt, appearing in photos to be a bit shorter than myself, had done the math on how much time he could save by reducing the ceiling height a few inches. As I continued forward stooped over, like Alice in the shrinking room, I realized that a few hundred yards was actually three or four years of hard work. Maybe Schmidt had shrunk so much from hauling out tons of broken rock that he didn't need the higher ceilings anymore.

It was dirty and dangerous work. From time to time, pieces of the mountain would fall on top of him. He'd dig himself out, and on more than one occasion, he'd limp toward a neighbor's house to beg a ride to the nearest hospital to get patched up so he could return to digging.

On a good day he might make a foot of progress. On a bad day, maybe only an inch. He added dynamite and ore carts to the mix, but still progress was slow and imperceptible. Day in and day out Burro Schmidt woke up, grabbed his pick, and attacked the mountain. He knew what he had to do, every single day, for decades. There must have been comfort in that.

A photo of him from back then shows a man with a crooked

back, pants filthy with grease, and a T-shirt ripped and full of holes. Still, evident even in a faded black and white photo, is the start of a smile. A look of pride in his sunken eyes.

In 1920, two decades into Schmidt's digging of the tunnel, a road was built over the mountain, making his tunnel useless. He didn't stop digging.

Maybe he thought he was close to finishing. Maybe he had come to love the rhythm and the purpose of the task so much that he could not bear to stop. In any case, he would spend another eighteen years digging the rest of the tunnel. Day in and day out, committed to finishing what he started.

As I go farther back in the mine, the light at the entrance reduces down to the size of a flashlight in the distance. I guessed that I'm halfway back. Halfway was nineteen years in Schmidt time. With nineteen more years ahead.

Then, on some otherwise uneventful day in 1938, having worked through the invention of the car and the television, through a world war, the Great Influenza, Prohibition, and the Great Depression, nearly four decades after he began, he saw sunlight at the other end of his tunnel.

His pickaxe, dulled and battered after nearly forty years of hammering away at the rock inside the mountain, clattered to stillness at his feet. A spark, a puff of dust. Newfound silence. He had chipped his way through a half mile of solid granite.

The exit was on the side of a steep cliff. There was a wash a few hundred feet below, but no practical place where the ore could have been transported from. Had he taken a wrong turn?

Had the whole thing been doomed from the start?

Schmidt was not the kind of man prone to existential questions. Soon after breaking through to the other side, he went back to the cabin he'd called home for forty years, packed up his few belongings, harnessed his two mules, Jack and Jenny, and left the place forever. No ore was ever sent through his tunnel.

But one man literally moved a mountain.

In my time at Cerro Gordo, I've come to view Burro Schmidt as the patron saint of the area and of my own undertaking. The tunnel that he dug, inch by inch through unyielding rock, is not a shortcut to nowhere as the cynics would have it. It is, for me, the most direct path through all the doubts and fears that have haunted me since I took on the task of rebuilding and restoring this decaying ghost town in the middle of the desert. Burro Schmidt's tunnel is a monument to what a person can achieve when they put all other considerations aside and push on toward a single goal. Heedless of the obstacles that stand in their way. Taking on a seemingly impossible task, not for profit or glory, but for its own sake.

I know this because I am standing in the testament to it. Many less foolish things, things that serious people took seriously, where are they now? So much has happened in the century since he finished, but the work, a bewildering but undeniable demonstration of human will, is still there.

Call it projection, call it wishful thinking, call it my own need to justify the seemingly insane decisions I made that led me to Cerro Gordo, but I believe Burro Schmidt died a happy man.

"The struggle itself . . . is enough to fill a man's heart," Camus wrote in *The Myth of Sisyphus*. I choose to imagine Schmidt as Camus's "happy Sisyphus." I choose to believe that Schmidt found joy and purpose in a task that others would find to be useless drudgery.

I had no idea such a powerful sense of purpose could be wrung from rock.

I do now. My road to that epiphany had cut through a few mountains, too. It led me to Cerro Gordo, a town just north of Schmidt's tunnel, with over thirty miles of mines burrowed underneath.

It was two A.M. when my friend, half-jokingly, sent me a message that said, "This might be your next project, lol." Included in the text was a link to an article: "Buy Your Own Town for Under a Million Dollars."

I clicked on the link, as I'd clicked hundreds of real estate links in my past, but this one wormed deep inside my soul.

The article included an aerial shot of a collection of sun-bleached buildings against a desert sky, as if Georgia O'Keeffe had freelanced a real estate brochure. In the distance, behind the shacks and sand, magnificent mountains loomed, the sort of things that excite the heart of a guy who grew up in the relentlessly flat suburban swamps of Florida. The town in question covered over three hundred acres, nestled in the mountains between the Sierra Nevada and Death Valley National Park.

It had a name that, while a bit clumsy in English, sounded beautiful in Spanish: Cerro Gordo—Fat Hill. It had been an almost legendary boomtown, a mecca for silver and lead mining in the 1800s, and some of the vestiges of its storied past still survived: a church, a few cabins, a hotel named the American, which had once been considered fairly luxurious for the location and the era, and a nine-hundred-feet-deep shaft into the old silver, lead, and zinc mines.

And then, there was plenty the town didn't have. No running water. No residents. No major stores for hours in any direction.

Despite the lyrical tone of the copy and the arresting beauty of photographs, it was clear that as fixer-uppers go, Cerro Gordo was in a league of its own. The kind of impossible place that could break a man's heart, his will, and his bank account.

In other words, it was perfect.

It was precisely the kind of challenge that I had been looking for.

My life at that point had devolved into a kind of numbing, comfortable sameness. When my friend sent me that listing, I was sprawled out on a worn and cozy couch on the front porch of a lovely 150-year-old Victorian mansion in Austin, Texas, that I had turned into a profitable and successful hostel, hosting travelers from around the world.

History and hospitality were, at that point in my life, my stock and trade.

But I was ready for a change, for a new challenge.

If I'm being honest, I was looking for the next thing to grab my attention.

If I'm being really honest, I was looking for something to hold my attention and not let go, the way that tunnel through the mountains grabbed Burro Schmidt. I just didn't know it at the time.

I grew up the son of two public-school teachers in the artificial uniformity of the suburbs outside of Tampa. In my house, education was important. Degrees were important. Going to college was a given, the question was what to go to graduate school for—a doctor, a lawyer, a banker. Solid, blue-chip jobs, the kind my parents would be pleased to boast about when the neighbors asked what I was up to. I didn't like blood, so being a doctor was out. Nor did I have the necessary tolerance level for boredom and bullshit to become a lawyer, so I focused on finance, where there was just as much bullshit but far less boredom. Where the blood that was spilled was almost always virtual.

I liked the perceived swaggering every-man-for-himself nature of finance. There was something about the sociopathic "coolness," the Gordon Gekko, Goldman Sachs, Patrick Bateman bad-boys of big bucks–ness that appealed to the eighteen-year-old me.

Deep inside, of course, I had my doubts. I was not, at least I don't believe, a remorseless me-first sociopath. But I tried to brainwash myself, watching a video entitled "Damn It Feels Good to Be a Banker" over and over, attempting to drown out the nagging pangs of conscience I felt but didn't acknowledge.

"I got a house in the Hamptons, and a penthouse loft . . ." rapped a guy in a suit pouring Red Bull into a Grey Goose bottle. Sitting behind my parents' house, entertaining myself by slapping the pond with a stick, the life of an investment banker sounded like an adventure. One that might even make my parents proud.

Simpler yet, grad school would give me an unambiguous answer to the question that nearly every young person gets bombarded with: "What are your plans after school?" I bought the ticket, and I took the grad school ride.

The dream came to an end in beautiful Gurnee, Illinois. I was there on a "due diligence consulting" gig pitched to me as a job in Chicago. Even after you get the job, banks can't stop sweetening the picture of what they do. My job, on this day, was essentially digging through boxes of unpaid loans and attempting to see how much the underlying asset was worth. A family wasn't making payments on their grain farm. How much could we sell the mortgage for back in New York City so someone could foreclose on the family and turn it into a Walmart?

The pay is good because the work is horrible. There was no Red Bull, no bottles of Grey Goose, either. Just two-for-one appetizers at the Chili's out front of a strip mall. I looked around the table at my peers five, ten years further along than me. They were slouched over their sizzling skillets, forcing small talk and waiting to die. How long could I do the job before I was just like them? If you don't take the money, they can't tell you what to do.

The day I returned to New York, I quit. I traveled. I ran out of money. I no longer had a good answer when someone asked me what I was doing. Neither did my parents.

I moved deep into Brooklyn into a three-bedroom apartment I shared with four people. I wrote articles online for $5 apiece. Graded standardized tests. Anything, everything, to not be an investment banker. Most of that money went to paying the debt for the schooling I wasn't using.

I felt stupid, yet free. Eventually I'd start a hostel in Brooklyn, which led to a hostel in Austin with its secret speakeasy and mascot goat. I met an author who introduced me to another author writing a book on marketing. I worked a day job in digital marketing (I still do) to pay for my side job of hospitality. Mastery comes from learning a variety of skill sets and combining them in a way nobody else can. That's what makes your specific skill set unique. I certainly wasn't a master, but I was learning what I loved and learning how to make a living doing that.

And then came that serendipitous late-night missive from my friend. A ghost town, smack dab in the middle of nowhere, a place I could revive and transform into a tourist destination, hospitality steeped in history.

I had just turned thirty, that magical age when, as a friend of mine once said, "no one will ever again say that you accomplished so much at such a young age" and the clock was ticking. I had by many measures found a successful life, but I couldn't shake the feeling that I needed something more, something that would demand that I tap into all the creativity I had. More than that, I wanted—no, I needed—a real life challenge, a test of my character, my abilities, my sanity.

I wanted to see what I was really made of.

The moment I saw the pictures of the place, I was flooded not just with excitement for the future, but also with a kind of borrowed nostalgia. Old memories flooded back of watching *Gunsmoke* with my grandfather. He lived with us for a bit when I was a kid. And he got me to watch his favorite show. I loved spending time with him and before I knew it, I was as enthralled by the adventures of Matt Dillon, Doc Adams, and Miss Kitty in Dodge City, Kansas, as he was. There always seemed to be a problem to solve, a bad guy to hunt down, riches to explore. Their fictional Dodge City existed in the same rugged era in which Cerro Gordo reached its zenith. I wanted to restore them both to their former glory.

I quickly learned that it's easier to find a dream than it is to finance one.

The property was listed for $925,000. Far more than I could ever afford on my own. If only out of curiosity, I called the real estate broker the next morning. I told him I wanted to make an offer. Maybe I'd get lucky and I could steal this out from under the noses of people who couldn't see what I saw.

"Get in line" was all he said. Apparently the listing had been sent around among lots of friends and they were already fielding hundreds of inquiries, including from the press, which only made the property a more competitive bidding situation. I didn't learn much in grad school, but I did learn what made a compelling real estate offer. Someone who had a vision. Someone who had passion. But more than anything, someone who could close fast. And to do that, I was going to have to convince a lot of other people to get on board to lend me their money. To do that, I was going to have to learn everything I could about this town.

I hung up and immediately dove into as much research on the town as I could find.

Once upon a time, Cerro Gordo was a thriving mining town in California's Inyo Mountains that extracted hundreds of thousands of tons of silver, lead, and zinc ore from the surrounding hills between 1865 and 1940. The many miners of Cerro Gordo produced so much refined silver in the first thirty years of the town's existence—roughly half a billion dollars' worth in today's money—that Cerro Gordo, 213.8 miles by road from the bottom of Sunset Boulevard—would come to be known as "the mines that built Los Angeles."

It was an important place during an important time in California's history. The more I read, the more I fell in love with it, and the more I wanted to go see it for myself.

As my car rattled into town, the vitality and significance that put Cerro Gordo on the map, and that jumped off the pages of all the articles I'd read, were a distant memory. In their place was the collection of dilapidated buildings I'd seen in the listing photo, most of them slouching earthward under the combined weight of 140 years of use.

From the center of town, standing on the splintered deck of a general store that had been turned into a museum, I could see the hotel with the saloon over to the left, built in 1871; the chapel down to the right, built in the second boom of 1910; a bunkhouse below that. Behind me, up a massive heap of waste rock pulled out of the mines, was the trestle of an old aerial tramway station, a building they called the assay office, and a large structure called a hoist house that sat on top of the mineshaft that went straight down into the mountain for nine hundred feet.

Surrounding the town core were a bunch of sunbaked cabins and about twice as many collapsed structures that used to be a hundred different things. They were all made with a combination of corrugated tin and old timber planks that had been scrounged and repurposed. Most of the buildings were uninhabitable. Many were full of junk. All were full of history, waiting to be told.

The buildings were connected by a network of roads and paths. Some were wide and smooth and looked like they'd been around as long as the town. Others were packed down and rocky, the exact width of a backhoe bucket. On either side of them, in between the buildings, was nothing but undulating expanses of dirt, rock, and scrub brush dotted with hunks of rusted metal that had once served the town—as ore buckets, ore carts, rail track, drill rods, and square nails—but were now just places for tumbleweeds to collect and for snakes to hide.

It was lonely and desolate, abused and abandoned, the most beautiful place I had ever seen. And I immediately fell in love.

Two main questions turned over and over in my mind as I walked the property: "How could I possibly buy this?" and "What could this become?"

Maybe it could be a kind of rugged Adventureland for grownups, an adult campground, with small, unelectrified cabins and safari tents, maybe some yurts. I had a friend with a line on some Airstream trailers. Maybe we could park those all around the property, and my other friend who is a fine artist could come up and give each one a unique paint job on the inside. Maybe we would renovate all the larger buildings and turn them into event spaces or meeting spaces and then rent the entire town out for corporate retreats and film productions. We could build stages against the hillsides and host conferences, too. Or maybe we could just let every piece of the place tell us in its own time what it wanted to be. As I went through all of the possibilities my mind was able to conjure, it was clear that whichever path I chose was going to require more than I was capable of.

But that didn't stop me from using pretty much every penny I had to my name, and a shitload of pennies from the bank and a group of friends turned investors to buy Cerro Gordo and become its newest owner. Much like Schmidt might have done in his day. The way most mines were financed in the silver boom—a dream and a handshake.

By some people's calculation, I had just committed myself to an incredible amount of risk. I had tied my financial fate to a dream that was defined primarily by uncertainty. Still, never once did I wonder, "How do I get out of this if the place becomes a money pit?" I never thought, "What should I do if all of these crazy ideas fail?" I only contemplated those first two main questions: What should we do, and what's it going to take? There is no playbook for bringing a dead town back to life, but given what had got me to Cerro Gordo, I felt just about as qualified as anyone else out there.

Mainly, I didn't want to become one of the mass of men, as Thoreau put it, who "lead lives of quiet desperation."

On June 13, 2018 (a Friday the 13th, of course), I officially took ownership of a "ghost town," with no way of knowing, not even a little bit, how much my life would change as a result. As much as I might have wanted it to be different, there is simply no way of projecting or preparing or planning for an adventure like this. Instead, like Burro Schmidt, I just had to grab my hammer, pick my spot on the rock, and swing. What other choice made sense?

Since purchasing Cerro Gordo, most of my plans have gone very awry. Every day is chaos with a side of adventure. There's been more than a few hospital visits. I've lost nearly thirty pounds since moving to the hill. I've lost a relationship. I've lost business partners. I've lost most of my life savings. Many think I've lost my mind. Many think I've wasted the best part of my "earning years" dithering away on an impossible task.

I wouldn't change a thing.

I came here as a city kid who couldn't tell a plumb bob from a pizza, but now I can build things with my bare hands, operate pretty much any piece of heavy machinery, survive in the wilderness, rappel deep into the earth and claw my way back up. I have battled fire and flood, earth and air, and I am still standing. And that counts for something. That counts for a lot.

There's a nineteenth century word for works of man that are remarkable for their achievement, for their ingenuity and the spirit of dedication that it took to create them, but which add nothing tangible to the world. As they cannot be commoditized, they have no practical purpose, and they're hardly the sort of thing a reasonable man would spend the best years of his life constructing.

They were called "follies."

CHAPTER 2

GET TO WORK

In a span of months after the end of the Civil War, an uninhabited patch of dirt became home to over four thousand people. More than five hundred buildings sprung up, including five known saloons, six hotels, twelve restaurants, three brothels, and a post office to boot. Cerro Gordo went from mountain to municipality in the blink of an eye.

For that to happen, every stick, every nail, every fixture had to be brought up on the backs of mules, who plodded their way up the serpentine "Yellow Grade Road" to Cerro Gordo as it climbed five thousand feet of elevation in less than eight miles. Every day, twenty mule teams finished their twelve-day trek from Los Angeles with supplies while another twenty teams departed Cerro Gordo with the valuable silver that would eventually turn L.A. from a pueblo into a metropolis.

If Cerro Gordo was a microcosm, one could say Los Angeles was a macrocosm of Cerro Gordo. Before the City of Angels had even had a chance to sprout its wings, this little city on a hill in the Inyo Mountains had already come alive. By 1870, in fact, Cerro Gordo was known as the home of the largest silver mine in the state. The governor of California visited. It's rumored Butch Cassidy, Wyatt Earp, and Mark Twain did, too. In those post-war years, if you found yourself west of the Rockies and you had money on your mind or adventure in your heart, the name Cerro Gordo was on your lips.

Then, sometime around 1930, in the midst of the Depression, the ore ran dry. And when it did, the town collapsed into ruin and decay.

Almost one hundred years later, in March 2020, I found myself stuck in a snowstorm, somewhere around midnight, halfway up that very same Yellow Grade Road. The world, and my world, were falling apart. A pandemic was sweeping the nation, closing cities, roads, and businesses—mine included. People were dying. Hospitals in New York had coolers outside of them to handle the excess dead.

I had just completed a marathon twenty-six-hour drive from Austin, Texas. I saw hospitals turning away patients in New Mexico. Roads closed in Arizona. I drove through an abandoned Las Vegas, with no visitors on the Strip, no casinos open, just ominous messages displayed on mammoth marquees like at the MGM:

"Stay safe and we'll get through this together."

"Ever apart, we're in this together."

"We can't wait to welcome you back."

I was headed up to replace Robert, the caretaker of the town. His wife was sick, he was sick of the town, and he had called to tell me he was taking off. Nobody would be there to watch the town once he left, so I had a decision to make.

Since the day we bought the place, I'd said Cerro Gordo needed to be my top priority. But living 1,500 miles away in Austin, I found a thousand and one ways to put the town on the back burner. We all dream of a life less ordinary, but what steps do we actually take to make that a reality?

J. P. Morgan once said every man has two reasons for doing anything: a good reason and the real reason. The good reason I was heading out to Cerro Gordo was to replace Robert. The real reason was to prove something to myself. That I could take more than just the first step in a big project. To my work, to my friends, to my life. I wanted a challenge that called upon all of me. To see what I was really made of.

I don't think I'm alone in feeling that way. I see it in many of my friends. We were brought up in this era where everything has been made easier for us, and so we got bored. Complacent. Disinterested. It's why cynicism has defined so much of our discourse. Our response to anything new has been "who cares?" Well, some of us have started to care. We want something hard. Something that makes us feel alive, feel purpose, feel connected to something larger. We want to prove to ourselves what we're capable of.

And when we see someone giving their absolute all to do that, to do something big that gives them purpose, it's the ultimate inspiration. It's proof of the possible. We're drawn to people like that. We're drawn to the things they do. It's why people pay to do Tough Mudder races. It's why we idolize Navy SEALs and fetishize their training methods. Or why TV shows like *Alone* are so popular. It's why the journey of Christopher McCandless into the Alaskan wilderness, his tragic end on an adventure that was in many ways doomed from the start, is, for some of us, both an inspiration and an admonition that continues to seize our imagination. Or why every rich tech entrepreneur eventually gets into hunting or Brazilian jiu-jitsu or ayahuasca. We seek out challenges. Voluntary hardships. Unimaginable risks. It's a push against the comfortable life we've grown to know.

Technically, of course, I'd already made that first big push against the comfortable life. I'd taken the first step toward doing something hard, something bigger than myself. I bought the town. My name was on the deed. Yet I hardly think I deserve any credit for that. Spending lots of money, especially when most of it isn't yours, is much easier than doing lots of work. If I wanted any credit for trying to make this dream come true, or for trying to build an extraordinary life, the first real step toward earning it, in my mind, was deciding to come out to replace Robert. The second step, it turns out, was making it up the road to even get myself there.

What is now called Cerro Gordo Road is a daunting, tricky beast. The first mile is the easy part. The road is wide. The curves, to the extent they exist, are long and gentle. The surface itself is flat—which is something, for an unpaved road made of nothing more than sand and crushed rock. Eventually, the mountain begins to rise up and pinch in on either side, and the road begins to rise and narrow with it. Very quickly the smooth ride disappears, and it feels like you're scrambling up an enormous wash that has been carved into the rock by centuries of snowmelt (which it has) then widened by force from decades of mule teams and heavy machinery coming up and down this pass in search of riches (which it was).

The middle stretch of road is pitted and rutted and off-camber. The remnants of large rockfalls sit within inches of your mirrors, a constant reminder that you're taking your life into your own hands when you choose to come up this way. The road's unpredictable shape has been defined as much by erosion as by usage, but with time you can get comfortable threading your way through these rocks. Then, as if out of nowhere, one side of the mountain falls away and you're left clinging to the other.

What you are left with, at least in the daytime, is something that will take your breath away: a majestic view across the valley of Mt. Whitney, the highest peak in the continental United States. From where you are on the road when you first see Whitney, it feels like you're eye to eye with the mountain. It is simultaneously enthralling and terrifying. The panorama draws your gaze toward it like a gravitational force. You just want to stare at it. But you can't. You have to keep your eyes on the road. Immediately ahead there are a series of steep, blind switchbacks to navigate, the apex of each covered in fine loose dirt churned up from extra wheel spin by a parade of drivers who danced on their vehicle's accelerator trying to get through the turn as quickly as possible. But not too quick. If you carry too much or too little speed into any one of these turns, it could send you over the side where the only thing capable of stopping your fall is the floor of Owens Valley, four thousand feet below.

It's only the last quarter mile of road that offers any relief to a driver's white knuckles. Even then, this is the stretch that is notorious for people getting stuck in the snow and the mud, just as the very top of town comes into view. It's a last cruel twist that Mother Nature applies to your journey as you arrive at a place she clearly does not want you to be.

I didn't heed her warning. I was too deep into my own sense of adventure. I hadn't even noticed that a storm was brewing, or more accurately, a storm was already raging a few thousand feet above me.

I was halfway up the road when a heavy, wet snow started to

swallow me. Thick velvety curtains of snow overwhelmed my cracked, old windshield wipers and erased my memory of the road's contours. My eyes struggled to distinguish between where the graded road ended and the sheer mountainside fell away. About a half mile from the entrance to town, I felt the truck's balding tires start to spin and its back end start to fishtail. The snow was getting too packed down and the road surface was getting icy. I had to stop. It was as far as my two-wheel-drive Tacoma was going to make it. I had no grip. To make matters worse, neither did my shoes.

I'd left Austin in a pair of the official shoes of the young entrepreneur: Allbirds slip-on "Loungers." Comfortable, simple, sustainable, and utterly useless in the face of even slightly adverse conditions. Like those shoes, I was ill-equipped for any of this. With night falling and the snow continuing to plummet, I abandoned the pickup with a bed full of supplies in the middle of the road, and hiked the rest of the way up the mountain in the least functional shoes possible.

My longing for adventure was still overriding any feeling of distress. None of these circumstances made me want to turn back. In fact, it solidified, in my mind, that I had made the correct decision in coming out. In coming to the town, I was hunting for an adventure. And I'd found it, even before I made it all the way into the town itself. I felt relief. Relief that I was finally doing something, anything to work toward my dream. I felt as though there was finally a purpose in each action. It brought every cell to life. Made me feel more alive than I had in the decade or so since entering the "workforce." I was carving my own path. I could barely sleep the first night, excited to see what the next days would hold.

I woke up that next morning to three feet of densely packed, wind-driven snow. Snow had accumulated around the truck, sticking it further in place. My tire tracks were covered over, too. Any sign that a living soul had traveled up the mountain the night before was gone. Not that it would have mattered. The road was now completely impassable. And if the National Weather Service was to be believed, it was going to stay that way for the next few weeks.

The idea of being marooned in the town for weeks because of even more snow made me even more excited. I wanted a bit of struggle. I wanted to experience the town, what people in the past might have experienced. I wanted the opposite of whatever my existence had been in my fancy apartment in Austin.

The historical reality of my situation hit me at that moment. For nearly a hundred years, men and mules died on that road I'd driven up the night before. They'd died building it, they'd died going up it and coming down it. Fortunes and futures died on that road. But they were made there, too, by people who had visions of a better life for themselves and got down to business making that vision real. There was so much potential in front of me, and I wanted to seize it. A similar feeling to what Mortimer Belshaw, the man who turned this patch of rock into a boomtown in the 1860s, must have felt when he first arrived in town.

Robert, the caretaker, was long gone, and nobody was coming to visit up the snow-packed road, so I took a walk—behind the main town, over the ridge toward Death Valley, where Cerro Gordo's Chinatown once thrived. Populated by hundreds of Chinese miners and merchants who'd immigrated in the 1850s to chase California's gold rush, this town within a town was booming by the early 1870s.

Despite the inhospitable landscape, there were multiple restaurants, markets, and dozens of dwellings made from whatever materials people could scrounge together. Today, you can still see the remains of a dozen or more of these structures. Most are just the stone cribbing of small enclosures built into imperceptible nooks all the way up the mountainside. On some of them you can see part of a wall or a doorway. One, you wouldn't even call a dwelling; it was more of a person-sized closet, nothing but an old exploratory mineshaft with a door nailed over the entrance.

In the two hundred or so acres that represented Chinatown, only one wood cabin remained. It was hidden down on a flat spot near the entrance to what I would later learn was the Newtown Mine, which protected it from a century of the harshest desert wind. Still, the cabin showed its hundred-plus years of abandonment. The whole structure leaned about twenty degrees to the right. Snow had blown in through the open door and through cracks in the roof, and it was doing its best to cover a wide porch out front that had all but succumbed to the elements. It was rotten to the point that to step onto it was almost certainly to step through it, down to the dirt below.

Still acclimating to the altitude, I stopped at the cabin to catch my breath and admire the view. On what used to be the porch sat an old stool that, somehow, over all these years, no one had seen fit to steal or break down into firewood. As I dusted the snow off the stool and sat down, I struggled to imagine what life must have been like for someone in this place—not just in the cabin, but here on the backside of Cerro Gordo.

A typical shift in the mines was twelve hours. You were paid $3 per shift above ground and $4 per shift below ground. An underground shift could have consisted of nothing but drilling holes in rocks, either by hand using a hammer and chisel, or maneuvering a massive rock drill. Maybe this guy wasn't so lucky. Maybe he was a mucker, and his job was to remove the still-hot rock from the end of a mineshaft after they'd blown a stick of dynamite. Maybe he was in charge of the timbering to make sure the mine didn't collapse on his coworkers. Or maybe he spent his days bending the track for the mine carts that removed the ore to the surface.

No matter what his job, it was definitely harder than mine. His anxieties weren't emotional or psychological or born from trauma like so many of my generation; they were literal and existential. They were about not dying from rock falls or explosions or drunken racial animosity.

In his free time he didn't have the luxury of dwelling on the past like we do, mostly because he probably had very little free time.

This cabin was evidence of that fact. After twelve hours down a mine, he needed to find shelter to keep the snow off of his head and the chill out of his body. If he couldn't find it, then he had to build it. So that's what he did. Then one day, you can imagine, after months on the mountain, maybe having saved a little money, he decided that he wanted a porch that he could relax on.

Nothing fancy. Just a little flat spot where he could put a chair, possibly a table, and maybe ponder his own big plans for those few moments he had to himself at the end of a really hard day. So he built that, too.

How much did it cost to build this? Did he actually spend time on the porch? What did he think about here, by himself, away from his family six thousand miles across the Pacific Ocean? Where did he go after Cerro Gordo? Did he go back? Did he have dreams? Did they come true?

I couldn't help but fantasize about the man who once called this place home.

The odd weight of falling snow accumulating on my shoulder

snapped me back into the present and it hit me that this porch and these cluttered, rundown buildings were a metaphor for doing big things, for making big changes. Each building here didn't go up like an Amish barn raising. The men principally responsible for growing Cerro Gordo into what it became didn't build the place all at once. It didn't come together as a singular, divinely inspired vision. They developed the mountain over a decade with their own money and muscle, one mine shaft at a time, one building at a time, stone by stone, plank by plank, nail by nail, silver ounce by silver ounce.

For almost two years, I had been telling myself we would restore all the buildings on the property. That we just needed to raise the money, hire the contractors and engineers, and then we'd get it all done in one big, frenzied crush of can-do spirit. Not a very good plan. We'd made precisely zero progress on it. We'd covered some of the costs from photo shoots or small events. But it wasn't sustainable. Dreams are great, but they have to sustain. And they don't sustain on hope alone.

The one thing fools all have in common, Seneca once said, was that they were always getting ready to start. In a sense, this is the question that life asks us all: When are you going to get serious? When are you going to get to work?

Until the answer is "now," you are a poser. That is an inescapable fact of reality, no matter how many pats on the back you get from your friends. So I said to myself, as Burro Schmidt must have said to himself one day in early 1900, that today was the day.

I will start with this cabin, I thought. Actually, no, I should start where the miner who built this cabin finished—the porch.

I figured I could probably put a porch together. It's a few floor joists, a step, some long planks, and a bunch of nails. When I was done with that, maybe the next day I could fix the split-open ceiling. It's basically the same principle as the porch—planks nailed onto support beams—just flipped upside down at an angle. After that was fixed, I could replace a few interior floorboards that had warped. And after that, maybe I could figure out how to fix the leaning walls, which was a slightly bigger job.

I'd seen the necessary materials for each of these projects scattered in and around a few of the buildings that were still in use. The chapel had dozens of planks of wood stacked up inside, for instance. I wouldn't even need to make the long trek down the mountain to the Home Depot two hours away. Not that I could at that point anyway. The road was packed with three feet of dense snow. Like it or not, I was here, and it was up to me what I was going to do with the time. If I did all this, bit by bit, day after day, at the end of it I'd have a structurally sound cabin that I could actually use. Maybe turn it into a writer's retreat, I thought.

With the snow now a thickening swirl of flurries blowing down off the ridge, I was overcome by this feeling that if I used my free time to do other small tasks around the rest of the property, then the big projects we'd priced out and budgeted for in our spreadsheets and investor decks might actually come together naturally. I hadn't done a single thing yet, so I was definitely operating on credit, but the simple fact that I could now see how things should work, and I was committed to doing them that way, seemed to open up a definable, walkable path toward making good on this crazy big dream.

I made my way back to town and headed for the chapel. I was riding high on ideas and wanted to get to work. I found an old cart and loaded it up with wood that looked, for the most part, like it was long enough. I tracked down some nails, a tape measure, a hammer, a saw, and whatever else was nearby that felt appropriate for rebuilding a porch.

By the time I got back to Chinatown, it was late afternoon and snow was falling steadily. It was the compact, icy kind of snow that falls with the angle of the wind and, if you're downwind like I was, hits you in the face like a bunch of tiny razors. I barely felt it. My focus was on roughing in the joists for the new porch, one at a time. Then it shifted to the dimensions of the porch as a whole. I decided it should be six feet deep and the full width of the cabin. For a brief moment I contemplated making it a wraparound porch, but I didn't know how to do that. It was too complicated, too many steps, too steep of a learning curve. I'd be thwarting myself before I even began if I gave this another moment's thought.

I put it out of my mind and started ripping boards with an old Makita saw. Feeling the teeth of the sawblade grab the grain of this old plank on my first cut, I could feel myself taking control of the future of the town. Before the day was done, there would be a new frame for the old porch in front of an abandoned cabin that was abandoned no more. It was a small feat in the grand scheme of things, but it was a start. A good start. The sense of pride I derived from seeing a space go from unusable to usable, the sense of autonomy that accomplishing this small task left me with, made me feel competent and effective.

That something, anything, had finally happened here, and I was the one responsible for it, gave me my first taste of the satisfaction that comes from working with my hands—from working meaningfully, diligently, patiently, incrementally toward a big goal. I had the urge, as scientist Edwin Land wrote, "to make a contribution that can be tangibly embodied . . . so that the individual hunts for a domain in which to utilize the urge." I was starting to find the satisfaction of finding the domain to utilize the urge.

A dream that is dependent on other people, on a bunch of conditions being right—that's a dream with no integrity. It's a hope, a wish, and not something to shoot for. It doesn't matter until there are boots on the ground, hands in the dirt.

As I drove the last nail into the porch frame, the snow had become so deep that I had to abandon my work before it became too difficult to hike the half mile back up over the saddle to the cabin I was staying in. I went to bed physically exhausted but mentally at peace.

Like Burro Schmidt, I knew exactly what I was going to do the next day. Get to work.

CHAPTER 3

WALK THE WASH

Things in the desert have a way of just disappearing, he told me. One day on a long hike he came across the most beautiful stone cabin he'd ever found. It was just over the hill from Cerro Gordo, not more than a few miles as the crow flies. But it was getting late and he was low on supplies, so he made a mental note of the place and came back to town. He would hike back out to the cabin the next chance he got.

"And I'll be damned if I could ever find it again," he confessed on one of our last hikes together.

"I've been searching for the past twenty years for that thing. But that's just the way things go out here. They disappear into thin air."

Things appear out of thin air in the desert, too. Not just things, but people.

The day Tip arrived, he did so in the passenger seat of an old Jeep painted in full desert camouflage.

Seventy-something. Small. Thin. Pale. Someone would later tell me he'd once weighed over three hundred pounds, but cancer had shaved off at least half of that weight. Thankfully it didn't steal any of his wit.

Tip was like a spirit. He only came when called, and only for those who sincerely needed him. I hadn't called Tip. I didn't even know he existed. But the town did. It had called him many times over his life, and from what I could gather he responded every time. This time would be no different.

Tip had no claim to Cerro Gordo, legal or otherwise, but the town had claimed him in such a way that his help was like the exercise of a spiritual fiduciary duty. No one knew Cerro Gordo or its thousands of surrounding acres like Tip did. Not just the physical land itself, but what had happened on that land. He was a geologist and a geographer, an ethnographer and a historian, an architect and an archaeologist. He was like the desert itself. Harsh and generous in equal measure. Simple and spare and mysterious. All of it beautiful if you knew what to look for, if you knew how to listen.

The first words Tip ever spoke to me were a command. "Get in," he said, pointing to a Bobcat tractor.

"Huh?"

"The Bobcat. It'll be faster."

OK . . .

"Left lever, left tracks. Right lever, right tracks."

I wasn't even in the Bobcat yet and already Tip was pointing left then right. There were mountains of debris from the fire that needed to be cleared. A bunch of volunteers with shovels wasn't going to cut it. And Tip, I think, wanted to see if I was going to take ownership of the situation.

It was the latest in a long line of opportunities since I had arrived in Cerro Gordo for me try something new, to learn something, to push myself. I jumped in.

"Go forward." I inched the Bobcat forward. "Good."

"Left foot, boom goes up." Tip pointed his finger up.

"Right foot, bucket curls. Do both." Tip rotated his hand to mimic a bucket curling up.

I made the boom go up, then curled and emptied the bucket.

"Good. Go get that stump." Tip pointed at a fire-scarred stump, maybe twenty feet away from us. Tip communicated like someone trying to save data on a limited text messaging plan. No wasted words.

Almost immediately I nearly flipped the tractor on its back.

"WHOA, WHOA!" Tip raised a fist in the air to signify STOP.

I regained control of the Bobcat and after a few awkward minutes of fumbling around, I had the stump in the bucket and had returned it to Tip, like a loyal retriever bringing back a ball to its owner.

"You're going to make a damn good operator," Tip said. "Just practice."

And practice I did. We had been lent the Bobcat for a week and I was hoping during that time to get the entire hotel site cleaned up. This meant six to eight hours a day in the Bobcat. I learned to float the blade to really smooth out a path. To shake the bucket when dumping dirt to make the pour more even. And bit by bit the debris at the hotel site disappeared.

I hadn't seen Tip since our first day of on-the-job training, but the day the Bobcat was due back to the tow company, I was up by the hoist house attempting to pour dirt over the area we'd just filled with all of the hotel's charred kitchen appliances. This required grading along a very steep edge with a twenty-foot drop beneath it. I was timidly scraping the dirt back from the edge when over my shoulder I heard, "It's just dirt. Don't be so precious."

Tip was back. He'd been watching me carefully grade the dirt for the past half hour.

"Hotel site's lookin' pretty clean," he added with a smile.

"Learned from the best."

"You learned from yourself."

Tip must have been feeling better that day. He offered to jump in and do some final cleanup before we had to take the machine back down the hill.

I watched him get in and attack the dirt with no fear. The boom and bucket were extensions of his arms and legs as he effortlessly tossed around tons of scree. Tip was getting more work done each minute than I did in ten. Still, every time he backed up I winced as the machine went completely off-camber. He was always one slight breeze away from tipping the thing over and sliding down the hillside.

And, of course, it happened. On a return run, Tip reversed into a massive piece of a charred stove that sat right next to the cliff that spilled over into a rocky abyss. I saw the line he was taking and tried to yell out, but he didn't see it and he couldn't hear me over the din of the diesel engine. One of the Bobcat's treads caught the edge of the metal stove and sent the machine's ass up into the air before tipping over on its side. I was convinced I was seeing the last of Tip, but luckily the tread on the other side of the Bobcat had become stuck on a different piece of kitchen equipment buried in the backfilled dirt, which kept the machine hovering there, teetering on the edge of disaster.

I ran over as Tip crawled out the side of the cab.

"Not the first time I've done that."

Barely an hour later, with the help of a few extra trucks, the Bobcat was back upright and Tip and I were sitting around discussing the best piece of construction equipment to get for Cerro Gordo, as if Tip hadn't just nearly plummeted to his death.

"See, the backhoe isn't really good at any one thing, but it can do it all. It's the Swiss army knife of heavy machinery." Tip was explaining that if I was going to really give it a run, really live up here full-time and rebuild, I was going to need a piece of equipment to literally do some of the heavy lifting.

I realized as he was talking that we both shared a common goal. We both wanted to see Cerro Gordo come back to life. It was the first time that I felt like someone else cared as deeply as I did about this project. I had owned Cerro Gordo for a while before moving here and meeting Tip.

Each trip up before then had left me feeling like a tourist in my own town. Tip talked to me as though I were a resident. Someone here to stay. He could hear it in my voice. See it in my eyes.

And he'd confirmed it for himself by witnessing the work I had done in the cleanup that week.

Tip didn't ask how long I planned on staying. He talked as someone who already knew I'd be here the rest of my life. He understood what was in front of me far better than I ever could.

"What are you doing tomorrow?" Tip asked, changing gears suddenly.

I was doing what I was always doing in those first weeks after the fire. More cleanup. He probably knew that.

"No plans," I said.

"OK. Ten o'clock, right here," he said.

"Sure."

"Make sure you've got water."

What he was asking, I was about to discover, was whether I wanted to take an adventure with him. Did I want to go on a hike?

Tip doesn't bring many people on hikes. He prefers to go alone. He's preferred to do most everything alone for most of his life. It's why the desert is a natural place for him. It's how he found his way to a career as a long-haul truck driver. Just him and the highway. It's why he worked at the Inyo County dump after he came off the road. Moving around people's garbage in a bulldozer was easier than dealing with all the crap that comes out of their mouths.

"I don't have the patience for most people," he'd told me.

Hikes with Tip were reserved for those who knew how to look and listen. Not to him, necessarily, but to the land. The land will tell you what you need to know. It will show you what you're looking for. It will show you when you didn't know you needed it.

I remember on one of our first hikes together, he stopped us halfway up a trail that only he knew of. It was on my property, and I had no idea it existed. I told him that. He smiled. When he'd found it years before, he let the brush around the trailhead overgrow so it would obscure it from anyone who he didn't think deserved to experience such a place. I laughed. He put his fist up. We stopped. He pointed in the distance, to a hillside no different from any others.

"See the trail?" he asked, knowing I wouldn't.

"The key is to turn your head slowly, from side to side. Keep your eyes on the horizon."

Tip demonstrated.

"When you see something that looks out of place, zero in there. Follow it to the left, to the right."

I rotated my head. Bit by bit, a patch of rocks that looked a little too straight to be formed by nature appeared at the bottom of my peripheral vision. I followed those rocks up the mountain, until another stack of rocks appeared, each one placed neatly right next to the other. Slowly my mind connected the gaps between the rocks until they formed what was once a mule trail. I saw.

Tip smiled as my eyes gave away that I'd found it.

He was right. When you learn how to look, you see. A lesson I would re-learn many times, including during one of our very last hikes. We were on our way to find another cabin Tip had lost track of long ago. As we came over a rise, that same distant hillside came into view, but the old mule trail was gone.

I pointed it out to Tip. He smiled. "It's there."

Tip taught me that time of day and even more so the seasons reveal different things about trails. The first snow will show patterns in the ground not visible in the summer. A trail that appears to end will suddenly be much longer, the snow clinging to the shale built up as cribbing.

I had last been on this trail with Tip in the late afternoon of a fall day and it was now a spring morning. The sun was in a different part of the sky now. A different height and a different angle. It shines on the rocks of that mule path differently in the spring. So you have to look at it differently, from a different height and a different angle.

I did what he said and looked carefully. There it was.

We kept moving. I wondered, how did he learn to do that? To see things differently. To see the same thing differently.

He peered down at me over his broken gas station sunglasses. His black leather belt was pulled extra tight around his jeans. The bill of his gray ball cap was pulled down, swallowing his face in shadow. I was struck by how small he was set against the mountain we were hiking on, yet how big of an impact he was having on the way I saw the world around me.

He gestured past me, down a ravine in the mountain. "Stone cabin. Lots of cans. Maybe more."

.He pointed. I didn't see a cabin. I walked, scrambling down the shale wash. The large, flat shards of rock moved under my feet like a river of broken dishes. It is one of nature's few truly unmistakable sounds. Like a wolf's howl. Or the whistle of a tornado.

The stone cabin was not exactly where Tip remembered. From the trail above, leaning on his walking stick he yelled "HIGHER," then "LEFT," then "BY THE DEAD TREE" as he attempted to access the location from his memory, which was still good, just slow to process these days. As the map in his mind began to resolve, or we simply ran out of other places to check, I started seeing more signs of human life.

An old sardine can with the lid still partially on it. A branch with a pipe grown into it, where someone once pitched a tent. A broken stoneware bottle from the late 1800s, where someone might have enjoyed a beer after a long day in the mines. They were all there, pooled near the bottom of this wash, carried there from decades of snow and melt.

When I finally saw the cabin, and was able to make my way over to it, I realized why Tip had a hard time remembering where it was. Not only was it unrecognizable now from wear and weathering, it was tucked into a stand of pinyon pines. Whoever built this place was trying to obscure it from undeserving prying eyes. Something I was sure Tip would appreciate now that we'd finally found the place.

The cabin no longer had a roof, half the walls had fallen in on themselves, and there were rusted cans all around it. Near the back corner I found an old tobacco tin and a small fifth bottle, buried just under the surface of a split floorboard. "The corner of vices," I thought to myself. Clues to a life once lived. To secrets kept. Crouching there, where I imagined a chair or a stool once sat, I looked out through the pines into the valley. It was a beautiful spot, defined by solitude and peacefulness.

I started wondering who had inhabited this cabin. What brought someone to the border of Death Valley to live in a crudely made stone cabin and eat canned sardines for dinner every night? Most likely mining. Or maybe one of the related trades. He could have been a woodcutter. Or maybe a blacksmith. What had his goals been? Was he running from something? Had he been happy? Had he appreciated this scenic view?

"WHAT'S IT LOOK LIKE?" The voice from above interrupted my daydreaming.

"NOT THE BEST," I shot back. "NO ROOF ANYMORE." I sensed myself mimicking Tip's short sentences. Trying my best not to waste any breath on unneeded words.

"10-4." Tip sat down under a tree.

After a few more minutes poking around and taking photos to show Tip, I started the hike back up the wash. Under the pine needles and shale, I found all sorts of other things. An old canteen, with part of the strap still on it. Another tobacco tin. A small piece of machinery. Half of a bucket.

I plucked them from the rocks. They'd be great for the "found items" part of the museum I was building out in the general store. There was more, so much more, but by this point my arms were full and I was having a hard time bringing just these new things back up with me. I was fighting gravity. I was also fighting nature. Things go down the wash easily; they are not meant to come back up.

"I took a few photos of the cabin," I said to Tip when I rejoined him.

"I've seen it before," he replied, ignoring the phone, more interested in the things I was carrying in my hands.

"All these came from the wash?" Tip asked knowingly.

"Yep."

"Yep." He smiled.

Spend enough time in the desert and soon you learn to read the landscape like an autobiography, or an autopsy. The washes that trace the contours of hillsides and mountain slopes empty into valleys and canyons—they tell you the history of every corner of the place. They show you how the blood used to flow. Where the water came from and where it went. When you walk them, especially up from the bottom, they reveal to you what flesh formed around this bloodstream, what life grew up around these waters over the decades, over the centuries, over the millennia even.

A wash isn't an old stream or a dried-up river, like some think. It's run-off. A record of where the waters from the heavens ran when the earth was full. In desert mountains, when the rain pours, when the snow dumps and then melts, the water always finds the path of least resistance down to its own level. That path is a wash. The fall line. And more than just water, it carries a thousand stories.

The things I collected from the wash below the stone cabin probably belonged to one man's story, but there was no way to really know. Tip and I went through the items, trying to conjure for ourselves an image of when each was used and why and by whom. Tip was the first to point out how cool it was that the sardine cans were cut open using a knife, so the cuts were jagged, not smooth like today's pre-cut cans.

"Imagine, a guy cut that open and that was it. Hasn't been touched since." Tip was getting more talkative as we dove into the past. "I bet he was a woodcutter. Did you see any old charcoal on the ground down there? Any stumps around?"

Tip started to describe to me the context clues to look for in mining country. If a camp was far away from any visible or known mine, it was more likely to have belonged to a woodcutter, who made his living chopping down trees and making charcoal for the furnaces in the larger neighboring mines.

"Sometimes you gotta kick around in the dirt, but you'll find the charcoal. Tough guys, those woodcutters. Back here all alone, chopping wood." Tip's voice trailed off. If you were the poetic type, you might have gotten the sense that this old man, wizened and weathered in his oversized shirt, cheeks sunken in by cancer, was looking for his own reflection from long ago in the image of those ancient tough guys. But Tip was not the sort of man who had much patience for poets. He stood up gingerly, leaning on his walking stick and a nearby boulder.

"People go all over the place looking for stuff. Let nature and gravity do the work," Tip continued, bringing the conversation back to the wash. "Just walk the wash. If you're ever in need of an adventure, just walk the wash." And with that, I knew it was time to head back.

As it happens, Cerro Gordo was likely discovered by walking a wash.

In the earliest days of prospecting in these mountains, the way to discover a pocket of ore that might be worth digging down for, was to look for "float." This was ore close to the surface that had broken off from its main body and floated down the mountain, typically in a wash, usually triggered by a combination of rain, rockslides, and earthquakes. A prospector would start at the bottom of a mountain, spot one of these washes, and start working their way up. As they walked, they'd keep an eye out for any rock that looked out of place.

In Cerro Gordo's case, the prospectors would have been sorting through limestone, sandstone, and shale, looking for galena, a much heftier rock thanks to its lead content that was streaked with color—dark gray, rusted orange and yellow, and a distinctive blue-green reminiscent of oxidized copper like the surface of the Statue of Liberty. When a prospector found one of those heavy rocks, they'd break it open (galena, like lead, is quite soft) and if the inside glittered, they'd know that somewhere above them was a deposit of silver galena. To find the deposit itself, they'd keep moving up the wash until the float disappeared, at which point they'd start looking to the left and the right of the wash, operating on the assumption that the absence of float meant the deposit was no longer above them. And if it wasn't above them, and it wasn't below them, then there were only two other directions to look.

With enough searching and luck, a prospector would discover a "surface deposit"—a pocket of ore that was visible and accessible right on the surface of the mountain. At Cerro Gordo, the two main surface deposits—the Jefferson Chimney and the Union Chimney—started at the surface and extended down 1,100 feet and 700 feet respectively. Those deposits, which were discovered in 1865 by a group of Mexican miners led by Jose Ochoa, Joaquin Almada, and Pablo Flores would turn out to hold the lion's share of the nearly $500 million worth of minerals that Cerro Gordo would come to be known for. All of it began with walking the wash.

Stories like the discovery of the Cerro Gordo deposits kept many men walking the wash up and down the Inyo Mountains for many years. Most of those men were on the hunt for riches, seeking their fortune. Others like Tip, and like me, as I was coming to understand, were on the hunt for something else. For a taste of the past. For context. For the experience of exploration, of learning about the land and decoding its story through the artifacts it shows us. That is what we seek. That is our treasure. Those are our riches.

Though I'm sure this wasn't his intention, Tip made me realize that the world is begging to be explored in this way. It's full of stories trying to be told, things trying to be found, knowledge trying to be understood. It's a series of interlocking puzzles waiting to be solved, hoping for one central question to be answered: What happened here? And Tip, for all his quiet, understated reserve, was the fullest example I'd ever seen of the human instinct to answer the call. When we'd talk and he'd trickle out bits of his wisdom, it became more and more clear to me that the only reason we know anything about anything—geography, medicine, space, you name it—is from explorations by people like Tip.

It was a jarring realization, because it flew in the face of the thinking that everything is just a Google search away. From the time I started middle school, this assumption was taken as the gospel truth. Anything you needed to know, the keyboard was the first place to go. And in our early experiences up at Cerro Gordo, that seemed to be the case. Google told me where the closest Home Depot was. It showed me where the Big Dipper was in the night sky. It taught me how to use Fix-a-Flat to fix a tire puncture. But Google can't tell you what to do with an abandoned mining town with no running water. It can't show you how to recover when the hotel that sat at the center of all your hopes and dreams burns to the ground. As predictive as the Google algorithm is, it doesn't know what knowledge or which skills you'll need on that particular adventure.

But Tip did. He was a veteran of the "sagebrush telegraph"—how word of mouth spread around the West. He knew about all the historic destinations in the area, ranging from old mines to campsites he'd found to trails nobody else knew of, which would make Cerro Gordo a very attractive hub of western mining history if I could get the hotel rebuilt and the water running again. He knew the people, too. He'd warn me about the types who would come to Cerro Gordo only for personal gain, not to do any real work. He'd give me the rundown on people in the valley to trust and those to look out for. He would never make any definitive statements. There were no callouts or takedowns. He'd only outline his experience and let me draw my own conclusions.

Tip also knew that no big project is completed alone. And I think that day on the mountain with the Bobcat, after a week of watching me grow with his teaching, he wanted to make sure I knew that I wouldn't be doing this alone. That at the very least he was going to be there for as long as he could be, to make sure that my proverbial toolbox was filled with the wisdom, tools, and skills I'd need on this crazy journey.

Even more than that, though, with months to live, no children, and the better part of his life spent alone hiking these hills, loving this town, and caring about what happens here, I think he was also looking for someone to pass on all his knowledge to. After all, the things Tip knew best—Cerro Gordo, the Inyo Mountains, heavy machinery, and the ways of old miners—were not widely sought after in today's world. Then here I come, new to the desert, new to the mountains, new to mining and to Cerro Gordo, in search of any advice I could get about how to make a go of it up here. I was the perfect recipient for all that Tip had to share.

When you start down the path of a massive project like Cerro Gordo, where there is so much stuff you don't know, it's hard to know who to reach out to for help. Or how. Or when. This is why mentors, teachers, elders are so important, and always have been. They've been where you are now, they've walked the wash, and they know to reach out first. To make their existence known. To make their presence felt. To make themselves available. They know what questions you're going to ask as well as which questions you should be asking. And if they don't know the answers, they know how to help you figure them out for yourself.

Tip was that person for me, and from the very first moment I met him, everything at Cerro Gordo became so much more possible.

CHAPTER 4

GO DEEP

There's a city under the town here. One that dwarfs everything on the surface, that rivals even the metropolis of Los Angeles

The mines twist and turn for more than thirty miles, buttressed by enough timber to build the Empire State Building out of wood a few times over. Deep enough to bury most of the Eiffel Tower.

There are elevators and chutes. Bathrooms. Changing rooms. Trash dumps. Dynamite vaults. I am writing now from a little alcove off the main mine, where a foreman might have checked his paperwork before directing his men to drive the shaft at the 400-level another twenty feet to the south. There is almost no sound in here. There is no breeze. No animals to make a sound, save the occasional bat. I love being in the mines. My phone doesn't work. Nobody can get ahold of me. The outside world disappears and I'm left to reminisce about the men who were here before. I'm transported back in time to think on the amazing property I'm able to spend so much time at.

Deeper still, there are railway systems and break rooms. There were stables for mules and pack animals that were born underground and never saw a single blade of living grass. Each day, hundreds of miners, entering at various points, reported for duty in this stone hive, this living, breathing mountain, chipping out this labyrinth of passages and secret chambers. Not everyone came home at night—not only because the mines ran 24/7—but because every few weeks, someone would die in an accident, sometimes many people all at once. Some are still there, entombed two hundred feet underground, walled off in tombs they dug for themselves.

Over the decades, a few thousand people worked in the mines at Cerro Gordo. Like World War II vets and men who walked on the moon, not many of them are left.

How many people have ever seen the mines that built Los Angeles?

The mines are the reason Cerro Gordo exists. Every single building on the surface, including the one I live in, was constructed to service the mines below.

Like a New York City banker traveling to work in their town car, it's easy to be so consumed with life above ground that you miss the subways and the ancient tunnels beneath your feet. It took me a few seasons to fully appreciate how deeply interconnected the world above and the world below are in Cerro Gordo.

The mining brought the town. To understand the town, you must understand the mines. To understand the mines, you have to get into them. And therein lies the rub.

Two years into owning Cerro Gordo, the extent of my mine explorations was tip-toeing a few dozen feet into the closest mine to town using my phone as a light. I understood conceptually that mines existed here, but with so much to see, so much to do on the earth's surface, I never gave it too much thought. I was more interested in what was happening above ground with the things easily in reach.

Which is what brought me to the old general store one day not too long after moving to town.

Built in 1866, the store was originally owned by a Canadian merchant named Victor Beaudry. Much like a German merchant named Levi Strauss operating at the same time three hundred miles north in the Sierra Nevada foothills, Beaudry sold all manner of provisions to hopeful miners—groceries, mining implements, liquor, tobacco, even fresh meat out of a butcher shop in the back. The general store was, both literally and figuratively, the center of town. There are photos from its heyday that show the building as the hub of the massive wheel that ground the mountain into ore, turned the ore into silver, and shaped the silver into cities. Within two years of the store being open, in fact, Beaudry and his partner, Mortimer Belshaw, would control more than half of that massive wheel thanks to a raft of unpaid debts incurred by miners who couldn't make good on their bills with the spoils from their claims.

Since serious mining operations ceased a century ago, though, Victor Beaudry has faded into history and his general store has been reduced to long-term storage. It has become a repository of all things past or unwanted. Equal parts museum and mausoleum. Generations of the town's few straggling residents shoved anything they didn't know what to do with into the back of this dark, dusty building. Artifacts, junk, paperwork, garbage. As each year passed, the piles rose higher and higher to the ceiling; they pushed farther and

farther out to the windows and the doors. The building had effectively become a time capsule.

Its many layers of debris and trash, like the rings on the stumps
of the gnarled two-hundred-year-old pinyon pines that dotted the
mountain, telling the story of Cerro Gordo in reverse, from its sad
modern languishing closest at hand on the outside to its golden age
as a great symbol of the West deep within its recesses.

By the time I bought the place, all light had been blocked out
from the back of the general store. Clearing it out had been written
off as an unpleasant chore, the reward for which would have been
driving truckloads of garbage back down the mountain to the nearest populated town of Keeler for disposal. No one had the time or the
inclination to tackle that job, the previous owner had explained to
me when I toured the property for the first time two years earlier.
With nowhere to go, I definitely had the time.

And with big plans for the town, I definitely had the inclination.

The first item I encountered was a garbage bag full of New Year's
Eve decorations from 2008. Then, a box full of *Sunset* magazines
from the early 1990s. I could easily imagine someone spending an
afternoon on the porch flipping through a spring issue and develop-
ing aspirations for a flower garden. I could picture them looking out
at brown, scrubby hillsides flecked by the tiny yellow and purple
buds of desert wildflowers trying to hang on long enough for the late
summer monsoon rains to come and unlock their blooms.

Hours later I had waded my way to a roll of muted orange shag
carpet, a clear indication I was now into the possessions of whoever
had owned this place in the 1970s. It took several days, but when I
finally reached the farthest back room, I found a display case with a

glass countertop that must have been used to sell tobacco and various medicinal elixirs back in the early 1900s.

Under the counter, wrapped in an old canvas blanket, was a briefcase. Around the turn of the twentieth century, a briefcase was an essential part of a person's life—it was impossible to conduct business without dozens of documents to buy things with letters of credit, to travel without letters of recommendation and proof that you were who you claimed to be. A rich man might own a briefcase made out of buffalo leather and brass, lined with satin or silk. This briefcase was made of wood and papier-mâché, literally dozens and dozens of compressed sheets of newspaper whose headlines and ads dated to a time when a fifth of whiskey cost sixty cents.

You're always hoping for treasure up here; undoubtedly that's what brought the owner of this briefcase up to Cerro Gordo more than a century ago. He was looking for silver and zinc. My hope was something else, something deeper: Maybe stock certificates to an old mining concern? Maybe a map to more mines? One of those old whiskey bottles could itself be a collector's item at this point. Some bottles, like old denim, could sell for tens of thousands of dollars if they were the right kind and in good shape.

I didn't find a fortune inside the briefcase. Instead, what I found was the life of a man named Chet Reynolds, told in bank stubs and love letters, court documents and bills. A treasure of a different kind. It was clear with every item I touched that Chet Reynolds had come to Cerro Gordo with two very dangerous things: hope and a dream. Holding up to the light one of his bank stubs from Bank of America for $8.43, I could feel his hope in the faded outline of numbers that were far too small, even for back then. Could he have ever guessed that, all these years later, a guy with a Bank of America account himself would be holding this record of his financial fate? Or that this same guy would one day buy for pennies on the dollar the town once controlled by vicious silver barons and opportunistic merchants who held Chet's actual destiny in their hands?

He couldn't have. Because his dream—the dream that brought everyone to Cerro Gordo in one way or another—had caught hold of him and blinded him to anything but the possibility of striking it rich. That's what big, crazy dreams do. They get you excited to the point where you only have tunnel vision. There can only be one outcome.

For Chet Reynolds, that meant following the veins of ore that flowed through the rock like rivers and waterfalls, no matter what it took. It meant following opportunities whenever they cropped up. Taking out mining claims all over the hillside of Cerro Gordo. Allowing the prospect of a better future to consume him.

It's estimated that of the three hundred thousand people who came west in the first Gold Rush in 1849, most lost everything and only a very small percentage got rich. Most of those fortunate souls were merchants and financiers, not miners and muckers like Chet Reynolds or the Chinese immigrants relegated to rock outcroppings on the other side of town. Ultimately, Chet Reynolds's dream, like that of so many miners at Cerro Gordo (or Tombstone or the Comstock Lode or the Klondike or the Sierra foothills), did not come true.

The bank stub was just the first clue. Then there were the notes. The first, from the Utah Junk Company, explained that his quarry was basically worthless. "With spelter at $4.40 at St. Louis I do not think it would be profitable for you to ship zinc ore so far." The second, from Dr. J Von Gal-Scale of Santa Ana, California, explained that on the off chance he made a sale of the worthless ore on Chet's behalf, he wanted his cut. "I figure, of course, on commission, which would be ten percent of what you get."

The ore did not sell. There would be no commission.

Mixed amongst Chet's financial records and business transactions were several letters to family complaining of long winters and growing snowbanks. There were lawsuits over unpaid bills at local supply stores. Then a bankruptcy, talks of shattered dreams, and a move off the mountain. And finally a divorce settlement from the Supreme Court of California. The petition for the dissolution of the marriage cited "extreme cruelty." I imagine it was the distance and the loneliness that doomed them.

This briefcase was a portable coffin for Chet's hopes and dreams. It was also a treasure trove of history, whose contents I found myself poring over, night after night. I was obsessed with placing him within the larger history of Cerro Gordo, which in turn got me fixated on the larger history of Cerro Gordo itself and the specific history of every little thing I encountered during my daily routine on the mountain. I needed to know everything. And the things I did know, I didn't want to forget. It would feel like a betrayal if I did, because that history was why I was here.

I had already started sharing a bit on social media about what I was doing up on the mountain.

But finding Chet's cache inspired me to start documenting everything I could.

I've always had completist tendencies. I remember when I moved to New York City for business school at twenty-one, I set a goal for myself to walk every single street in Manhattan by the time I graduated. I bought a map of the city, taped it to my bedroom wall and every night traced with a highlighter the streets I'd walked that day.

Each day, a new bit of the map came to life. It was no longer black-and-white street names and intersections. I knew the smell of each part of the city. The lights. The history of how each area came to be. References in music, literature, conversation, all meant that much more. When Cam'ron rapped in my headphones, "I'm from 101, west a Hun'fortieth," I could see those streets intersect in my mind. I lived fifteen minutes from there. It wasn't just words anymore, it was a living color picture.

I saw where the Harlem Renaissance happened and where Dylan got started and the brownstone where Theodore Roosevelt was born and the stairs where Washington was sworn in as president. I walked through the Meatpacking District, then known for its world-famous nightclubs, and saw slaughterhouses and packing plants still there. The smell that still existed in the cobblestone roads. I stood silent and stunned at the African Burial Ground near what we now call Tribeca, the forever home of thousands and thousands of slaves, ghosts of a New York that New York tries to forget. I walked the High Line—then a new, fashionable park—and learned about its origins in the 1920s with Robert Moses. Which led me to read *The Power Broker,* which helps one to see the city as a series of political battle-grounds, neighbors as winners and losers, victims and victors. I wasn't just passing through someone else's domain, I was co-existing with them. My experience living in the city was so much more rich.

The world around you comes alive when you pay attention to it like this, when you care about it, when you dig deeper to understand it. And once you do, that's when you come alive, because you've al-lowed for a connection to something bigger than yourself.

When you're able to form the same level of connection to your work, your project, it all means so much more to you. The work itself is much more satisfying.

Back in Cerro Gordo, tucked under Chet's briefcase in the general store–slash–museum was a yellowed copy of a United States Geological Survey (USGS) report from the 1960s that laid out in fine detail the true extent of the massive mine complex that had been sitting unexplored right under my feet since buying the place. Its many sketches and diagrams, along with descriptions of areas that surveyors couldn't get to, were like a map to a lost land that I immediately felt compelled to learn everything about. To gain that feeling of belonging, of meaning. It was my new map to pin on a wall.

I had to walk the same mineshafts that the founders of the city had, as I did in New York. Get down in the tunnels that Chet Reynolds had walked, feel the same cool, dark air that he had breathed. Rappel down the areas I couldn't walk to. Push aside rock if it stood in the way. Walk the city under the town created over a hundred years ago. Reynolds was the composite for every other miner who went up to Cerro Gordo, lived and died, and never left even a briefcase to remember them by. I wanted to understand them, I wanted to understand Chet.

I needed to get inside the mines. So when the USGS report describes "a 6-foot white quartzite bed which probably lies stratigraphically . . . near east and tips 30° to 42° S" between the 550 level and 120 sublevel (page 55), I know exactly what they meant. What the white quartzite looks like. The galena (lead and silver) Belshaw was looking for above and below it. What L. D. Gordon, the man who ushered in the second "boom" to Cerro Gordo with zinc, sought out years later. How it connects to everything else about the town.

I would finally fully grasp all the stories I'd read about old prospectors like Burro Schmidt and Chet Reynolds. I was searching for meaning, for greater context for this wild adventure I was undertaking. I wanted better insight into why I was so obsessed with seeing this place come to life.

The low-hanging fruit was picked first. Any mine that was easy to access I walked into. The first day of the mission, I must have ducked into more than a dozen mines. I was sprinting toward understanding. Trying to make up for my ignorance of what was just below my feet. As more and more sections of the map became colored in after exploration, the most daunting remained—the Jefferson Chimney.

The mines are the reason Cerro Gordo exists and the Jefferson Chimney is the reason the mines exist. The Jefferson Chimney is the most important (and at one time most valuable) sliver of land for hundreds of miles in any direction.

A "chimney" in this case refers to a vertical ore body that starts at the surface and runs vertically down. Imagine a crack in the earth, sometimes hundreds of feet wide, filled in with valuable minerals. It's estimated that more than half of all the ore that came out of Cerro Gordo came out of the Jefferson Chimney. The Union Mine itself was sunk where it was to access the minerals running deep in the Jefferson Chimney to the south and the Union Chimney to the north.

Yet, until I came upon the USGS report, the existence of the Jefferson Chimney was unknown to me. It was the mother of the entire town, and even after marrying the town, not only had we not met, I didn't even know she existed.

Reading deeper into the USGS report, the enormity of the deposit became clear: The Jefferson Chimney "having been mined from the surface to termination below the 900 level" (page 57).

Meaning at one point in time it was mined all the way from the surface down to nine hundred feet. Meaning the Jefferson Chimney would touch every level of the Union Mine. Using the main access shaft to the mine, I had run into collapses on almost every level. If I was able to access the Jefferson Chimney, that might mean I could access those levels behind any collapse. Meaning many more miles of mine to explore.

As I flipped through the pages of the report from 1963 to learn more, the author summarized his findings as such: "Except for the small surface pit, all workings in this channel were inaccessible at the time of the present study." Inaccessible. The most important part of the entire town, inaccessible. Deep into my race to understand it all, that sounded much more like a challenge than a definitive statement.

One hundred and fifty years after they started mining it, the Jefferson Chimney is a terrifying crack in the earth that appears to descend forever, situated halfway up Cerro Gordo's peak.

The chimney, from high above, looks like a slash in the earth's crust. Somewhere around ten feet wide and fifty feet across, the opening is covered on either side by large rocks sticking up on the mountainside. It's completely invisible for anyone searching for it from below. The rocks obscure the cut. If you happen to be hiking down the mountain, the chimney makes itself known right when you get to the edge, and nothing separates you from a fall to an imminent death.

The same loose rock by the edge tumbles into the abyss as I lean over the edge.

When the author of the USGS report, Charles Warren "C. W." Merriam, deemed the Jefferson Chimney "inaccessible," he was mostly right. Inaccessible without nearly a thousand feet of rope, harnesses, lights, and a general lack of fear.

Sixty years after publication, I was back with the necessity of rope, a full body harness, industrial descenders and ascenders, and a determination to see what was in the Jefferson Chimney. In my backpack I had extra flashlights, MREs, a gallon of water, an airhorn in case of emergency, and Merriam's report, rolled up for reference. I didn't know what to expect. As I crept close to the edge of the hole, my mind reeled. I reminded myself that once upon a time I had been afraid of heights. Maybe I still was, but that wasn't enough to stop me. There was history to be discovered. If the literature was correct, it had been mined at least nine hundred feet down. An exploration down there could take days, weeks, even.

Peering down, there seemed to be no end to this massive pit. Just weary old timbers, the size of full trees, gamely straining to hold the crack in the earth open. It was a warren of suffocatingly tight squeezes interspersed over a seemingly bottomless drop. I took a deep breath.

"All right, I'm just going for it . . . So, see ya," I called out to my safety partner watching the rope above. You can't let the intrusive thoughts win; sometimes you just have to go. And with that I lifted the handle on my descender and started sliding down the rope, my feet desperately flailing out, my toes trying to grab hold of any rock in front of me. The entirety of my weight supported by a rope that always looks a bit too thin, tied around the base of a sagebrush bush (there were no better anchors in sight). The feeling of dangling from a rope, with no idea when your feet will touch solid ground again— even recalling it now, my stomach does backflips. I'm not sure I'll ever get used to it. But I love it, in a way a skydiver likes jumping out of planes. Sometimes in life you just need to let go.

About thirty feet down, my feet touched rock. A ledge, not visible from the surface. Off the ledge was a short tunnel, the edges of it jagged from the hurried dynamiting that gouged it out of the rock. This was nowhere in the USGS report and not available in any other literature. History already being made. Ten feet into the tunnel was a dynamite storage room, complete with wooden dynamite boxes with a few dozen red sticks of dynamite still packed, sawdust and all. There were no signs of life. No footprints in the dust covering the floor of the shaft, not even from animals. This was virgin territory, and I was only fifteen minutes into the exploration. My mental understanding was growing. I wasn't just consuming the history, I was adding to the record. My camera rolling, I excitedly read off the top of cans I found, "California Cap Co."

"All right, I'm going down again," I yelled up, as my descent into the unknown continued. I was riding high on the thrill of rappelling, of discovering new history, of feeling alive in the space I love so much.

A series of claustrophobic tunnels with broken and rotten ladders followed. I had always been thin, but I had shed 30 pounds since leaving Austin, and even still, I struggled to squeeze through the narrow tunnels. I was twisting and turning through sharp rock no wider than four feet. I could not see more than ten feet below me, leaving me to only guess where this snake hole was taking me. This initial part of my journey was entering the access point to the chimney. Here, the miners wasted no dynamite making the hole larger than it needed to be. This was a transport path to the main show. As I played chutes and ladders inside an increasingly dark setting, my rope tangled around the jagged, sharp rocks, left behind by the dynamite blasting of the ghost that inhabited the void.

Finally free, the room around me expanded dramatically. Bobbing there, attached to a rope braced against many sharp rocks, my life in the hands of the small metal teeth of my descender.

I must be in. This must be the famed chimney.

I narrowed my light beyond my legs—it shined its farthest without giving up the bottom of the shaft. I wiggled the rope below me—it swung freely as if the end was still mid-air. The edge of the crack where I entered was no longer visible. I could no longer hear the chatter of those who had come to watch me go down.

I lowered myself further. Now hundreds of feet down in the mine, I was starting to trust my equipment with my life. I reminded myself of the weight capacity of the rope (over two thousand pounds). I reminded myself how many people go rock climbing each year without incident (more than ten million in the United States alone). I, for a very brief moment, felt incredibly free. In awe of the situation. I was venturing to somewhere nobody had gone in a very, very long time. I was facing my fears head-on. And most important, I was connecting more deeply with the property I had grown to love.

The daydreaming, and descent, all came to an abrupt halt.

"What the fuck," I let out to the void. I was no longer descending. All my trust I had finally relinquished to my equipment I gobbled back up. I was stuck. My sleeve had become caught in the teeth of the descender, not allowing me to go down, yet not allowing me to go up either. I was stuck, mid-rope, with an unknown fall below me, and hundreds of feet to ascend back up above me.

Do not panic. If you think of nothing else, think of that first when in a life-or-death situation. Do not panic.

I stopped fighting with my sleeve and allowed myself to swing on the rope for a moment. Below me, what I had now dubbed the "pit of despair" loomed. A few deep breaths later I unhooked my ascender from my belt, clipped onto the rope, raised myself to the point where I was able to untangle myself.

I began to lower myself again, this time a bit slower, acutely aware of the situation I was in.

Eventually, my feet hit rock. Long before nine hundred feet, and not too long after the sleeve situation, I found myself standing on solid ground, next to an even bigger pit of despair. The pit I was descending down was maybe fifty feet wide. This new room opened up to be hundreds of feet tall and over a hundred feet across. It was a small auditorium, hundreds of feet underground, created by carving the valuable ore out of the earth.

A stope. That's what the miners called these large open spaces created by extracting ore. This was the largest stope I'd ever seen. By going deep I'd opened up a whole new world. I realized that this massive opening in front of me was the actual Jefferson Chimney. What I was standing on was the 86-level of the mine. A part of the 86 that accessed the ore body. A part of the 86 that is inaccessible from the typical mineshaft because of a collapse halfway back. I had roped in behind the collapse and was accessing a part of the mine not seen in . . . 108 years.

I knew it was 108 years because not far from the larger pit of despair was a powder magazine (a room where they stored dynamite). Inside one of the wooden Hercules dynamite boxes was a scrap of newspaper with a date—May 5, 1913. Likely the last time someone had been in this part of the mine. That particular box was empty except for what appeared to be dirt. If you're wondering why there might be a newspaper next to an empty box filled with dirt deep inside a mine, I'll remind you that these men worked twelve-hour shifts underground. I'll allow you to fill in the blanks.

The discovery of this connection of the Jefferson Chimney and the 86-level is not one shown in the USGS report. It's not one mentioned in any of the literature on the area. I was blessed, once again, with the joy of discovery. Of a feeling of belonging to the world around me.

Unfortunately for me, after zigzagging through the maze to get to the 86, I did not have enough rope (nor stamina) to continue down the new pit of despair. I explored what I could, documented my findings on film, and decided to pick up the exploration another day.

As I explore, as I document, everything I do feels more consequential. Every mine I wiggle into, every artifact I add to the museum, every building I start to rehab becomes imbued with more meaning, which means they become more meaningful to me. And together, that gives my life more meaning because it puts even the most laborious tasks I have to complete in a larger historical context. It makes my dream less about me and more about the town and those who will, hopefully, come after me.

The joy of discovery that comes with exploration has always been a powerful force in my life.

Once I got to Cerro Gordo, and that force was animated by a desire to increase my understanding of the place so that I could preserve it and share it with people, it became a guiding light. I followed the joy and focused on the history because I knew it would clarify why I was here and deepen my appreciation for the work left to do. I think it can do the same thing for anybody working on a big project or a big dream.

In fact, I think that kind of clarity and appreciation is necessary, especially when you consider how recent generations—mine included—tend to think about doing big things. They design "disruptive" products or technology like they're wiping the slate clean. Like they're starting over. They behave as if the past doesn't exist or doesn't matter. Nor the future, either. The number of founding stories I've heard that begin with an exit plan is more than I can count. All that does is bake impermanence and irrelevance and obsolescence into things. It makes dreams disposable. That can't be good.

In the pursuit of big dreams, an appreciation for the past, for those who have walked the wash before you, helps you understand where you fit in the grand scheme of things. It shows you that you are part of a lineage, and that there is wisdom and guidance to be had from those who built that lineage. It gives you someone to look up to and something to live up to. When you're having doubts, it gives you inspiration. It makes you part of history, and that is a position worth protecting and embracing. Even when things go horribly wrong.

WATER

You don't know the worth of water till the well runs dry. That's what the old men say. They never tell you about the feeling you get in the pit of your stomach when it's gone, though.

They never tell you about the icy dread that grips you when you know—deep down and on a cellular level—that the water has stopped flowing. You can't understand it, not until you've felt it.

I knew it before I was even awake this morning. I don't really know how I knew. Maybe it was the silence. In an old house you never notice the sound of the water when it's running, any more than you hear your own heartbeat, the muffled hisses as it trickles through ancient pipes, the drips from an old faucet on the far side of the house. But when it stops, the silence is deafening.

The dread that comes to you in that silence is even sharper when you've known the want of water before. In my time here, I've felt the weakness, the confusion that comes when you're dangerously dehydrated. I've gagged on my own tongue when I couldn't even raise enough spit to swallow. Ever since I arrived here, in this place of extremes, I've known that I was always just a few drops away from disaster, and that anything, a prolonged drought, a sudden flood that washed away our primitive attempts at infrastructure, a blizzard or even a sudden deep freeze, could destroy everything I've worked to build.

The temperatures plummeted last night. The last few drops of water in this desert town froze solid in the pipes that lead to my house. Maybe they'll thaw when the sun comes up. Maybe those pipes, worn out and exhausted after more than a century of abuse, won't split wide open when they do, spilling the last of my precious water onto the parched scree outside my door. But even if they do thaw, it won't matter. The water tank that feeds them from above is empty.

You don't know the worth of water 'til the well runs dry. And when it does, it's a feeling akin to grief. I'm in the bargaining stage now. I'll make little deals with the universe, or at least the clouds above the desert. I'll skip my small comforts, I won't shower, I'll let the dust of Cerro Gordo calcify on my skin, I won't do dishes, and I certainly won't try to trek to the top of the mountain where the last cache of water lingers. I wouldn't make it anyway, not even with the skid-steer. As if to taunt me, the mountain has let just enough water ooze into the crevices of the rutted mountain road to turn it into an icy slalom, making it impassable. Insult to injury.

I'm not the first man to stand right here, in this spot, and pretend that my petty sacrifices will appease the water and cajole her into flowing again. As long as there's been life in this desert, it's been at the mercy of her caprices.

As long as there's been a Cerro Gordo, it's been perched on a knife's edge, teetering between water and want. I think about water all the time here. You can read the record of its cycles of plenty and pain everywhere. You can see it in the sun-bleached skulls of bighorn sheep I find from time to time while hiking on the mountain, proof that sometimes this land will provide enough water to survive, in some years, enough to thrive, and then just as quickly, it will vanish.

It's always been that way, I suppose, due to an accident of nature, of geology. Twenty miles to the east, the peaks of the Sierra serve as a kind of barrier, greedily sucking up moisture to sustain its lush forests, preventing much of it from reaching the desert. But even there the evidence of the cycles of water is plain.

You can see it when, in a parched season, the dry ground below the tree line becomes too weak to hold the shallow roots of the tall pines and they topple over. The tree rings tell the tale.

In the years when strong storms blew off the Pacific Ocean and lowered above the Sierra, the rings grew wide and healthy. And in the years when it rarely rained, the rings grew narrow and frail.

Sometimes, when I look across the valley at those distant peaks, and think of the lushness of their forests, and imagine the sound of fresh, clear, trout-filled streams, galloping over rounded, mossy river rock, I get covetous. I'm not the first man to have felt that, either.

Covetousness is a crime, a crime committed against this place, and the evidence of it is written in the nearly dry bed of Owens Lake that lies between the mountains and me. Back in the days when Cerro Gordo was thriving, that lake was teeming with life and brimming with water. In the town's heyday, hundreds, thousands of acre-feet of water was hauled up from the lake and into town on the backs of mules, one canvas water bucket at a time, where every miner and merchant cheerfully handed over a shiny ten cent piece for every gallon. By the 1870s, a few enterprising entrepreneurs located a hidden spring not far from town, and piped the water in. They cornered the market on water. Prices plunged and giddy miners immersed themselves in it. Literally.

According to contemporary accounts, there was actually a run on soap and bathtubs when the spigot was turned on in Cerro Gordo, as grimy miners joyously discovered the luxury of bathing.

But the lush times didn't last. They never do. The desert is a trickster, and cruel. In due time, the spring ran dry. Within a year, the miners and their bone-dry bathtubs had been painfully reminded of the worth of water.

Springs fail. Rains refuse to materialize. That's always been true. And for ten thousand years, across the parched landscape of human history, we've found ten thousand ways to adapt, to engineer a solution, even if only by the seat of our pants, to the crisis created when our wells run dry. We're an inventive species, but we're also a covetous one, and we've never found a way to channel or stanch our greed.

The consequence of that failure is etched in the parched, sunbaked mud of what used to be Owens Lake. Make no mistake, it was human greed that drained that lake, greed personified by one of the most ruthless characters in American history. His name was William Mulholland.

He was, in his time, regarded as the father of the modern city of Los Angeles, a veritable Moses who struck his staff on the rocks of the desert and brought forth enough water to slake the thirsts of nearly four million Angelenos.

But up here, some regard him as a common thief, and the dried lakebed is the chalk outline at the scene of one of his crimes. I'm not sure that view is correct, either.

CHAPTER 5

LONG-TERM CONSEQUENCES OF SHORT-TERM THINKING

"There it is, take it."

Snow had fallen the night before, and the morning light danced on the white blanket on the distant mountain peaks. There's something about the silence that comes after a snow. It gives you time to think. To admire the way the snow hones the light to a knife's edge. It makes you believe that you can see forever. From where I stand, I can see the entire outline of what was once Owens Lake.

It's hard to imagine, looking at it now, but once upon a time, Owens Lake covered an area four times the size of Manhattan. It had lain there, cradled between the snow-capped peaks of the Sierra Nevada and the Inyo Mountains, undisturbed for twenty thousand years, ever since the retreating glaciers carved its bed out of the rock and filled it to the brim with cold, clear water. It was a sanctuary and a source of life for everything that ever lived in this desert. Massive flocks of birds would circle the sky, blocking out the sun before they descended, in formation to the shore.

Twice a day, at dawn and again at dusk, deer, bears, wolves, would make their way to the water's edge. The Shoshone and the Paiutes, people who understood at their core the worth of water, would make pilgrimages there, to ease their thirst, take their share of the legions of fish that swam in the deep blue waters, and hunt the uplands that rise from the shoreline.

Even after the immigrants staked their claims in this place and built a boomtown out of their dreams of riches, the placid waters of Lake Owens rarely had to suffer any greater indignity than the occasional barge, laden with silver or provisions, chugging across its surface.

Standing here now, seeing the lake so diminished and degraded, a ghost lake at the foot of a ghost town, I try to convince myself that maybe, in the grand scheme of things, it's better this way. If that lake were as vital and alive as once it was, then Cerro Gordo might now be Tahoe, an oasis in the desert for the affluent, its rugged shoreline ringed with second homes torn from the pages of one of those old *Sunset* magazines I found, and not the place I've come to love.

But I can't help but feel a sense of loss anyway. Tinged, perhaps, with a touch of anger.

"There it is, take it," were the words of William Mulholland, the superintendent of the Los Angeles Water Department, who in the early 1900s devised a plan to "take" all of the water out of what was then Owens Lake. And so they did. Using all the foul alchemy of early twentieth century technology, they wrested every drop of water they could from this pristine lake, manhandled and channeled it and ran it downhill to the Los Angeles basin, leaving little behind but the sun-bleached bones of what used to be Owens Lake. And they were celebrated for it. The bad guys won.

It's almost mythic in its treachery. The silver pried from these mountains helped make Los Angeles powerful, and when she was powerful enough, she came back and sucked the lifeblood out of Cerro Gordo. The water.

Was it theft? Who knows. There was certainly a victim.

We are who we have always been, a greedy species; silver, air, water—we take what we want and call it "discovery" or commerce. They say there is barely a single fluid ounce of water on the planet that wasn't here at the beginning of time in one form or another, and the entire history of our species is shot through with tales of the strong poaching water from the weak. "Whiskey's for drinking, water's for fighting over," or so Mark Twain said. I don't know if he said it before or after he visited Cerro Gordo. But he was right. And it's a zero-sum game.

Los Angeles County, a cultural and economic powerhouse that is home to nearly ten million people, a sprawling factory town where they manufacture our national id on Hollywood backlots, owes its very existence in no small part to Mulholland's "discovery" of Owens Lake and places just like it.

I wonder if Mulholland felt the same sense of awe that I conjure when I try to imagine the lake as it was when he first set eyes on it, one hundred square miles of water stretching toward the horizon, two hundred feet deep in the wettest years. Probably not. The superintendent of the Los Angeles Water Department in the early days of the last century was, by all accounts, a practical man, not given to sentimentality or emotion.

Mulholland had come to this valley because he was trying to

solve a problem. The burgeoning city had almost outgrown the freshwater resources available to it. The city had met its limit on growth, except nobody told that to all the people starting to move there after the turn of the twentieth century. Like a shark, the city had to keep moving forward, or it would wither. And so Mulholland and his longtime friend and mayor of Los Angeles Frederick Eaton spent over a decade scouring the backlands far away from the city to find a new source of freshwater for the parched city to support its continued growth. They found what they were looking for in Owens Lake.

Water is often a dirty business, and Mulholland and Eaton did not mind getting in up to their elbows. Almost with a kind of perverse pride, they used every trick they could come up with to cajole or con or coerce anyone who they thought might stand in their way. They sent agents into Owens Valley disguised as wealthy cattle ranchers looking to acquire land, and with it, access and rights to the surface water. At the same time, they exploited connections with local newspapers to raise a panic that a drought was looming and that it would dwarf the droughts that had come before. They had bet that no word is more terrifying to desert dwellers than the word *drought,* and that a steady drumbeat of warnings above the fold every week in the local gazette would cow the landowners into selling their land and selling it cheap. They bet right. And soon enough, Mulholland and his crony held the deed to most of the land in the valley. Only then did they finally reveal their plan to the locals to move the water more than two hundred miles away to water a garden of earthly delights in somebody else's backyard.

I sometimes think of those old photographs in glossy movie magazines from Hollywood's Golden Era, muscled leading men and starlets lounging on chairs beside the shimmering water of a swimming pool, surrounded by lush, live oaks, at their Beverly Hills estates, never wondering for an instant where that water came from. Why would they? It wasn't in their script. It was another spoil that came their way in a wonderful dream life.

They don't issue death certificates for lakes or for any natural resource. But if they did, the death certificate for Owens Lake would be dated November 5, 1913.

That's when the water from Owens Lake started flowing downhill. And life would never be the same, for either place. Los Angeles would become, well, Los Angeles. Owens Valley would become a dustbowl. Within a matter of years, everything in the valley would shrink and wither, and the valley itself would become a plundered colony that merited no attention.

There was resistance, of course. But it was the kind of desperate resistance that comes from people who understand that water is indeed for fighting and that they've already lost. On several occasions, local ranchers, on the verge of extinction and outraged by Mulholland's deception, dynamited the aqueduct, most notably on May 21, 1924, when five hundred pounds of dynamite were detonated just north of Lone Pine. According to well-watered officials in Los Angeles and the governor's office, it was an act of domestic terrorism.

By 1926, Owens Lake was completely dry. Before long, the naturally occurring metals and elements that had once been safely diluted by the copious waters of Owens Lake were now dangerously concentrated and baked into the dried mud in the lakebed, creating a toxic hazard that spread far and wide every time the wind blew up a dust demon. It got so bad that in the 1990s, Los Angeles appointed a special master charged with returning an infinitesimal amount of water to Owens Lake to control the dust. He was dubbed the "Deputy of

Dust." It has a nice ring to it, doesn't it? I never met the man, of course. But when I imagine him, I imagine him holding his handkerchief over his face and hacking up clods of dust everywhere he went.

There were decades of lawsuits that followed, costing the taxpayers of Los Angeles more than $2 billion. The lawyers are still billing; the toll ticks higher still in every sense. As screenwriter Robert Towne later said, "When a crime can no longer contain or content itself with the past and insists on visiting the future it's no longer a crime—it becomes a sin, and very difficult to punish."

But in the end, up here, all that was left was the desiccated cadaver of a once thriving ecosystem.

It's always there. I see the scene of the crime from my bedroom window when I wake up in the morning. The consequences of it define my early morning routine. I stare at it as I walk to the outhouse. We still use those here. The water that could have been pumped up the mountain instead watered lawns beneath the iconic Hollywood sign a few hundred miles away.

Even today, "toxic" and "costly" are the best way to describe the relationship between the two places. Inyo County is still locked in a bruising legal battle with Los Angeles to determine how much more water the city has to give back to the area. At the same time, Los Angeles still owns over 250,000 acres, or about 89 percent, of the private land in Inyo County.

And corruption still plagues the department that William Mulholland once ran. In July 2019, the FBI raided the offices of the Department of Water and Power, along with the city attorney's office. The charges ranged from bribery to fraud on the part of top DWP executives, one of whom pleaded guilty to bribery and lying to the

FBI and was sentenced to four years in prison. Old habits die hard, I guess. Everyone, it seems, is still paying a price for the rapaciousness of LA's forefathers.

And yet, it all could have turned out so differently. The randomness of chance always depends on who is holding the dice. Who knows how things would have turned out if Mulholland had never "discovered" Owens Lake. Maybe there'd be a city here and I'd be prowling a ghost town at the foot of the San Gabriels. Maybe both would have prospered. Maybe neither would have. What is clear is that Mulholland's scheme was an inflection point, and it sealed the destiny of both places.

In 1870, at Cerro Gordo's zenith, the town boasted nearly four thousand residents. That same year, Los Angeles had a population of 6,500. The towns were active and equal trading partners, peers almost, and much of Los Angeles' prosperity was due to the miners from Cerro Gordo. For them, the dusty little hamlet on the coast was a convenience. San Francisco had deeper mining roots and sturdier infrastructure as a port city, but it was also much farther away and mule teams would have to traverse more dangerous and inhospitable terrain to reach it. When time is money, you go with the closer option. That was Los Angeles. Smaller and less mature than San Francisco, it was still a port city from which hungry miners up on the mountain could source supplies and sell their silver.

Cerro Gordo sent so much to Los Angeles that a Los Angeles newspaper wrote in 1872, "To this city, Cerro Gordo trade is invaluable. What Los Angeles now is, is mainly due to it. It is the silver cord that binds our present existence. Should it be unfortunately severed, we would inevitably collapse."

You'd think they'd have been grateful. You'd be wrong. When the silver ran out, so did the grace, and Cerro Gordo was forgotten. Until Mulholland "discovered" it anew.

"There it is, take it."

By any means necessary.

In the surprisingly candid and frank film *Chinatown*, Mulholland's cinematic alter ego, Noah Cross, in a conversation with a private eye named Jake Gittes, imperiously excuses every sin he ever committed in pursuit of water and other things and justifies condemning one place to a dusty death for the benefit of another, with two simple words. "The future, Mr. Gittes! The future." It is as accurate a depiction of true history as Hollywood has ever produced.

At seventy miles an hour, the wind is hot and dry enough to turn your skin to leather, but all the same, I shift up to see if I can coax a few more clicks out of my engine as I skip my dirt bike like a stone along one of many rutted roads the DWP has worn into the arid lakebed during their decades-long battle against the dust.

Something is missing. I don't think there's a word for it. There ought to be. It's a feeling that most motorcyclists are familiar with, something that you don't feel on foot—the changes are too subtle— and that you never feel when you're insulated in a car. You have to be exposed to the open air to sense it, traveling at speed, but when you find yourself near water—an ocean, a lake, a pond, even a mountain stream—you feel it before you see it. You feel it deep inside, a kind of quickening.

I hardly feel that anywhere in this surreal moonscape where the lake used to be.

Rolling back the throttle, I pause to take in the scene in front of me.

Owens Lake hasn't just been killed. Its corpse has been defiled. What remains isn't even the broad, flat uninterrupted ghost of an inland sea like you might find at the Bonneville Salt Flats. Here, in a last-ditch effort to hold back the dust, lines of ditches and mounds have been carved into the earth across vast swaths of the lakebed. The engineers quaintly call them "moat and row" structures, as if they've borrowed them from an English country garden. They look more like those sepia-tinted photographs you see of breastworks on a World War I battlefield.

Elsewhere, in those places where the naturally occurring salts are so highly concentrated that they could kill off even the heartiest desert plant, gravel has been strewn, a few inches deep.

The idea is to entomb the dust, to bury it and forget it.

Between the trenches and the tombs, the DWP has simply tried to beat the dust into submission, roughing up the surface of the soil in hopes that it will reduce the speed of the wind when it comes barreling through the valley, similar to the way a mangrove hammock breaks the relentless rhythm of the waves on a seacoast. Eeriest of all are the fields of irrigation sprinklers, misting the sunbaked soil with warm water. It's an exercise in futility. All around them the ground remains as white as a bleached bone, shrouded in a thick mantle of a substance that looks like coral.

Visiting the lake is visiting another world. And apparently, I'm not the only one who thinks so. Back in 1989, when the dreammakers from Hollywood were casting about for a place to represent the desolate and uninhabited planet of Nimbus III for the film *Star Trek V: The Final Frontier,* this is where they came.

But here's the thing about nature. It's stronger than you'll ever be, more resilient. There's a reason why every culture in every corner of the world has, embedded somewhere in its myths, a story of death and resurrection. It's because we've seen the evidence of it from the beginning of time. Cycles of decay and renewal are etched into the DNA of every plant and every tree and every animal. And if I turn off my engine and really look, I can see it beginning here. Green shoots at the edge of the lakebed, reeds that tempt wary migratory birds to return and stake a claim and nest here. In those few remaining puddles, flocks, sometimes huge flights of waterfowl, will gather. It's rare, and they don't stay long, but they do come, and every time they do, I like to think that nature is flipping William Mulholland the bird.

I'm not the first man to find and nurture a glimmer of hope in the few surviving pools left at the bottom of what was Owens Lake. Back in 1969, a man named Phil Pister was walking in Owens Valley and he stumbled on a small natural spring. There, swimming in it, glinting in the relentless sun when they dashed close to the surface, were the very last of the Owens pupfish, a creature found nowhere else on Earth. They had long been thought to be extinct, wiped out when Mulholland drained the lake. Researchers stumbled across a few remaining survivors, but they were rarely seen, and the final extinction seemed inevitable. To everyone except Pister. Excitedly, Pister grabbed two buckets, filled them with water and all the pupfish he could wrangle, and with that, he single-handedly saved an entire species.

Fifty years later, the pupfish species still survives. Pister, alas, does not. He passed away in 2023 in his nineties.

But cheating defeat is not the same thing as victory. And the question remains, despite Pister's valiant effort to pull the pupfish back from the brink of extinction, what happens next? Where can they go? With their ancient, evolutionary habitat destroyed by colonizers from Los Angeles, is there anywhere they can be safely returned to the wild?

Maybe it's fitting that at this point, the pupfish's fate may lie with a people who have their own painful history of exploitation at the hands of colonizers, who themselves faced possible extinction. The Bishop Paiute Tribe has offered its reservation as a wildlife refuge for a fish that nobody else seems to care about.

For all its lost beauty, and all the awful beauty of its current degraded state, for all its history, it's things like the saga of the pupfish that for me make Owens Lake an object lesson in the lethal danger posed by our snatch-and-grab culture. As individuals, as communities, as a nation, we are a people who have been conditioned to demand immediate gratification, the consequences be damned. It's as if we've lost the ability to think in the long term, to measure our short-term wants against the needs of all those interdependent systems that support us. "There it is. Take it" ought to be inscribed on our coins instead of *E Pluribus Unum*.

Our past is our past. We cannot change that. But we can and do form our futures, and it's well worth asking whether by exploring the road not taken, by examining all the might-have-beens, we can chart a better course to what still might be.

For example, where might Los Angeles be if Mulholland and Eaton and their supporters had not been laser-focused on the easiest possible solution to a difficult problem? What if those men had looked over their shoulder to the west instead of casting covetous glances two hundred miles eastward? What if they had been content to share instead of steal? What if, back then, they had invested their time and money in finding a way to leach the salt out of the sea, a practice that dates back to ancient times when Greek and Phoenician and Roman sailors would kindle fires on deck to distill seawater and make it potable? Los Angeles could perhaps still have fueled her growth and been the global leader in a new technology, desalination, which is now being deployed in water-starved Texas, and in the Middle East, and in overpopulated Florida, which are fast outpacing their fresh water supplies; indeed, everywhere in the world where a changing climate and an exploding population are draining the cisterns. Los Angeles could have been on the cutting edge of that technology. Now it's playing catch-up.

Would they have been able to achieve it in those days? I don't know, maybe. The first days of the twentieth century were marked by an unprecedented boom in human inventiveness, for good and for ill. Those were the years in which we first learned to fly, and in which, in a desert here in the Southwest, we first tested nuclear weapons, which now could wipe out every living thing on the planet. Would it have been risky? Yes. Would it have been expensive? Definitely. But calculators were $1,000 when they were first invented; now they give them away in cereal boxes.

If our history—distorted as it is—has taught us anything, it has shown us that nothing is impossible. With time and patience, with long-term investment and a clear vision of the long-term goal, anything is possible, and once it's in the world, everything becomes more affordable—financially, historically, and cosmically.

I fire up my bike and wheel my way back across the corrugated bottom of the long-lost lake, and in the droning of my engine I begin to ruminate on all the other things we've lost since Mulholland first turned up here.

We've lost generations of people who could have been building something lasting, something real, the last of those generations devoting their energies to designing ridiculous apps, not because anybody really needs them, but simply because they imagine that if they appeal to the right demographic they can sell them for millions or billions of dollars to another company, retire before they're thirty, and spend the rest of their lives, like those studs and starlets in the old movie magazines, lounging around pools in some Southern California enclave, filled to the brim with water that shouldn't be there.

It's like a virus that has spread through the entrepreneurs of my generation especially. Instead of searching for something they care deeply about, something that would give to others and in the process give them a sense of purpose and meaning, they are reacting to the sharp shock of micro trends the way a dead frog twitches when you hook up an electrode to it, and asking questions like, how do I get a million users, now? How do I get to a billion-dollar valuation, now?

How do I get my dinner, my package, a ride to the airport, an answer to my question, now now now now?

Move fast and break things—that was the internal motto of Facebook—and now seemingly everything. Disruption. Disintermediation. These are the buzzwords of today's economy . . . buzzsaws of destruction, of externalization. Yes, something broke, very badly.

You want to be able to hail a cab from your phone or get dinner delivered? It's a wonderful convenience that only a fool would deprive themselves of using. Your wish is my command. But just try not to be too disturbed by the plight of all those gig-economy wage slaves as they serve you, working long hours without benefits, without a safety net, emitting, polluting as they drive individuals—or their Thai food—around in Los Angeles traffic, door-dashing any hope that we'll invest in better public transportation.

This need for instant gratification, for immediate solutions, for convenience on command, of catering to the individual, it breeds impermanence and exploitation and disposability. And all of these "innovations" carry with them massive, long-term consequences. Some are unpredictable, some are all too predictable, and some are consequences that we're already feeling and struggling to deal with.

I'm not trying to be some holier-than-thou hermit, some noble Luddite hiding out on this mountain. I'm just asking for some forethought. I am well-aware that I'm able to stay here and continue to build here because I was able to tie into a Google-owned company that has allowed me to build a community of people who have become deeply and personally invested in our progress here. Digital media has allowed me to build a global network of support that has benefited me personally and has benefited Cerro Gordo practically and financially. But that has only been possible because through it all, on my pages, and in my posts, I have tried to keep my focus, and our supporters', on the long-term goal.

Cerro Gordo is in the predicament it's in now because of short-term thinking, its own and others'. In a way, the town was built on the shaky foundation of short-term thinking. By definition a mining camp is a place where nobody thinks more than a few years into the future. No mining camp ever built was expected to last more than five to eight years, ten at the max. "There it is. Take it." Get in, get out. The last one out douses the kerosene lamp. But before you go, strip what you can, take what you can use, and pawn off the rest.

That's what happened at Cerro Gordo. In the days after the mines proved to be tapped out, old owners would sell artifacts for $5 a bucket. Wood from the original hotel was sold to the local pharmacy for beer money. Cabins were dismantled and sold, as people continued to scrape every dollar they could TODAY, not thinking toward the future. The men and women who built this place were never married to the land. For them, it was a kind of one-night stand, which in geological time meant it would last about ten years. There was no commitment.

But there is comfort in commitment. There's freedom in it, too. I'm not sure that I ever articulated it, even to myself, but what I was always searching for was the big project, the big dream, the great goal way over the horizon. I wanted the freedom that comes when you bind yourself to something, the freedom to think long term, to embrace the big picture. When I started this, I thought that maybe, just maybe, I'd found what I was looking for in the real estate listing for this decrepit old ghost town. Now, years in and still swinging the hammer, I know I have. And for all the hardships, the setbacks, and the frustrations, I don't think I've ever been happier in my life.

I wonder if Mulholland would say the same if he could stand at the edge of Owens Lake today, would his hollow chest swell with pride to know that his stamp on the environment is still so visible over a century later? Would he, like Noah Cross, justify the exploitation of Owens Lake with a couple of curt words and a nod to all the prosperity it brought to Los Angeles? Or would he have been filled with remorse, the way Alfred Nobel was years after inventing dynamite, or Robert Oppenheimer was immediately after the first successful test of the atom bomb?

I suspect not. The magnitude of the problem he solved and the complexity of the plan he conceived to solve it were so grand, I can't imagine he would see his contribution to the history of California as anything other than a net positive. If he likened himself to a character out of myth, it'd probably be Prometheus, the bringer of fire, and not Shiva, the destroyer of worlds.

This may surprise you, but I'm not sure I would think differently were I in his position. You can, as I do, detest Mulholland for his perfidiousness, and loathe him for the consequences of his deeds, and still be amazed by the feat of engineering he achieved. To have had the vision to look at the snowpack around Mt. Whitney and think, "There it is, the secret to my city's future," and to be able to then turn that vision into a stone-cold reality was not only audacious, it was brilliant. To give the devil his due, what Mulholland achieved here was Pharaonic in its scope, at once awful and awesome.

"You see, Mr. Gittes," Cross says in *Chinatown*, "most people never have to face the fact that at the right time and the right place, they're capable of anything."

CHAPTER 6

WATER FROM A STONE

"There's water down there."

Nothing steals one's attention like talk of water in the desert. Especially at Cerro Gordo, where there's almost never been a reliable source. So the town has relied on trucking up all the water it needs. But there is one tantalizing, almost mythical solution . . .

"A lot of water."

Tip wasn't talking of the kind of water that sometimes gushes and sometimes trickles down a wash or snakes along the backside of a mountain. Those are fickle and undependable in the desert. No, he was talking about the motherlode, a rich cache of water vaulted deep down inside the mountain, seven hundred feet below the surface, where water seeps in through the sides of the shaft.

A few hundred yards below me, there may be all the water I thought I could ever need. A few years into showering using wet wipes, using outhouses in freezing weather, and deciding my meals based upon how many dishes they would create, Tip had my full attention.

But of course, there was a catch.

The water was seven hundred feet down the original mine shaft. The only way to access it was by using "the hoist."

A hoist sounds like a very technical piece of equipment, but fundamentally it's an elevator with no buttons. This particular hoist, built around 1910, is effectively a giant winch, a massive, forty-foot-wide rusted steel wheel, a spool wrapped in hundreds of feet of equally rusted braided steel cable, which was itself attached to a rickety steel cage, open on the sides, basically nothing more than a platform. In the old days miners would clamber aboard that platform, and the operator would fiddle with the dial, sending them down into the mine, 86 feet, 200, 400, 550, 700, all the way down to the 900-level. The miners would then load their day's take onto the platform, and it would be hoisted back up. It had never been particularly trustworthy as machines go. And time and disuse had made it even more suspect.

But now I had to accept the fact that the rusted steel cable was my lifeline. Reliable water would fundamentally change the experience at Cerro Gordo. Later, we'd need a much larger catchment in order to adhere to the fire codes required to rebuild the hotel and we'd bring up the forty-thousand-gallon water tank. But in this moment, the promise of a reliable source of water was worth whatever effort and risk was called for.

To get to the water Tip was talking about meant that I was going to have to trust my life to a wheezing machine older than my great-grandfather, dangle above a nine-hundred-foot drop, and hope for the best.

A lot of good men have gone down into the Union Mine. A good number of them never came back out. The stacks of newspapers I've found in the general store tell the stories of the deaths and accidents that happened down that infamous hole. A collapse in the 1870s that killed thirty-five Chinese miners. An incident in 1877 in which a man fell down the shaft to the bottom and the *Inyo Independent* reported he "was found a shapeless mess" at the bottom. Or that day in 1872 when a man "fell down from the four hundred to the seven hundred foot level. His body was horribly mangled." One does not go that far down without grave personal risk.

Making matters worse, in the hundred years since the Union was actively mined, faults have shifted, tunnels have collapsed, and the mine itself is more dangerous than it was when all those headlines were written. It's been at least thirty years since anyone risked riding the winch to the bottom of the mine. Probably for good reason.

Literature and scripture are full of stories of those who descended into Hell and returned to tell the tale. Dante, Persephone. Greek and Roman mythology is filled with journeys to the Underworld. Odysseus, Hercules, Theseus, and Aeneas, just to name a few, all went to obtain tangible or spiritual wealth—could be a treasure, could be the Sorcerer's Stone or the One Ring, could be a friend, a lover, a piece of wisdom. The descent sometimes included some drama, but as Aeneas was warned before his descent in *The Aeneid,* "the way down to Hell is easy . . . but retracing your steps and getting back up to the upper air: there is the task, there is the job!" If the hero is lucky, they return with whatever they went seeking and something they weren't expecting: a heightened sense of what they are capable of.

Tip had been to the pit of Hell, decades ago, and had managed to trace his way back to the land of living.

When he told me that he had seen the water with his own eyes, I believed him. Tip wasn't one to embellish things. He was no myth-maker. Especially at this point in his life; he didn't have time for frivolous adventures. He knew that on my journey to restore this town, water was the missing puzzle piece. And he was convinced that there was not just water down there, but that we could get it.

"I know some guys."

I paused. Then nodded. "Let's do it."

Tip started making calls and I started making plans, more excited than I had been at Cerro Gordo in a really long time. Dreams of hot showers overpowered any hesitation.

On the day of our descent, it became clear just how risky an adventure we were undertaking. Peering deep into the mine from the entrance with a flashlight, we could see how much damage time had done. Here and there, timbers had fallen into the shaft over the years. The guide rails that sent the cage down were warped and looked like the undulating tracks of a roller coaster.

Even if we could get the hoist operating again, we would have to somehow navigate it past tight spots in the rails, and past the loose two-by-twelve timbers that were lying across the shaft, threatening to impede our descent. Removing any one of these timbers could affect the structural integrity of the entire shaft. One loose board could mean a dozen loose rocks could mean a collapsing shaft.

We didn't know how far down the cable could go. We didn't know if the cable was frayed at any point or if it would even unspool from the massive drum it had been coiled around for the last three decades. The hundred-year-old pipe that brought the water to the surface was made of galvanized iron. That meant that it probably hadn't rusted over the years, but it may well have split in places, or been torn by shifts in the mine. There was, allegedly, an electric pump down there that had been used to coax water to the surface, but we had no way of knowing whether it was still there, or whether someone had hauled it up and sold it off for parts. Even if it was still there, there was no guarantee that it would work. Ancient electricals don't usually fare well over the long haul in deep, dank mines. It would, almost certainly, have to be replaced.

Any one of those challenges could, on their own, dash my dreams upon the rock at the bottom of the mine, leaving them, like that old miner in the newspaper story, a "shapeless form."

Aware of the risks, appreciating the stakes, and understanding the obstacles in front of us, a "dream team" of locals started to develop around me right there on top of the mountain.

The first guy I met from what would become the "water crew" was Craig Leck. An easygoing guy in his early forties with a full head of salt-and-pepper hair, Craig is an electrician by trade who lives down the road in Independence. From the neck up he looks like someone who could have been in John Wayne movies. He has piercing blue eyes and a neatly trimmed goatee that sits below a meaty, slightly crooked nose that looks like it may have seen the business end of a pipe wrench at some point in his younger years. He's the kind of guy who you know the minute you shake his hand that he knows how to make things work. You can just feel it in his grip.

Though he looks and sounds like he's been here forever, Craig is also a pilgrim. He grew up in Los Angeles, but spent his recent adult years in Owens Valley. In me, I think he saw a bit of himself. A guy from a city who'd fallen in love with the pace of the desert and had to find a way to belong here. Craig had spent enough time in the valley to know all the major forces down there. He had two jobs. Outside of having his own electrical company, he also worked for LADWP, the bureaucratic heir to Mulholland's legacy. He worked mainly with concrete on the aqueduct, but he was also the department's general "fix anything" guy. Over his years there, he'd learned a thing or two about water, the valley, and how to get things done.

Next was Dave Mull, the owner of the NAPA Auto Parts store down in Lone Pine. Dave's store functioned as much as the town water cooler as a parts store. When you needed to fix your car or fix your thinking, you went to Dave's. Because of his bearing and his position of authority behind the counter, he has become kind of the unofficial mayor of greater Lone Pine. He's a formidable figure. Tall and broad-shouldered, with a wild gray beard that unfurls behind him like a battle flag when he roars through the desert on his Harley-Davidson motorcycle. You always get the sense that he's taking the measure of everything, and when he peers at you over those old, tinted wire-frame glasses of his, it's sometimes hard to figure out what he's actually thinking.

I've gotten to know him well enough now to understand that he's here with us at the mine in part as an official function of his unofficial position—he needs to see for himself what's going on. But he's also here because he wants to find a way to help, including locating and supplying parts to get the hoist running and to make it safer.

And then there's Tip's partner in crime: John Bowden, a man he had been exploring the valley with for nearly thirty years. John was a former marine with long gray hair, narrow deep-set eyes, and a tight smile that made him look like a cross between Sam Elliott in *Road House* and Kris Kristofferson, or at least Kristofferson's alter ego in the song "The Silver Tongued Devil and I." John is in his sixties now, with a house down in Keeler, a wife named Roxanna, a retro-modded Jeep with a full desert camo paint job, and a talent for telling tales that are always just true enough. If Dave Mull was the unofficial mayor of Lone Pine, John considered himself the former mayor of Cerro Gordo, and he had no problem letting you know.

John and Roxanna had once been the caretakers of Cerro Gordo in the early 2000s. They knew the property as well as anyone. He claimed to have been down to the water at some point, as well, but he couldn't exactly pinpoint when.

Rounding out the group was a bear of a man named Cody, who was a crane operator for LADWP. Cody was good friends with Craig and Dave and given his experience with cranes (and his sheer size to pull back the emergency brake if needed) he was an obvious choice for the hoist operator. In charge of sending the cage up and down, he would literally have our lives in his ursine paws when the time came to start sending us down.

The first step was making sure the hoist would actually work. Dave had some extra parts down at NAPA, so he outfitted the hoist with a hydraulic braking system in an attempt to at least make our adventure a bit safer. Once that was installed, the operation of the hoist was fairly straightforward: Release the giant locking brake to free the spool, pull down on the lever to make the cage go up, push up on the lever to make the rusty old cage go down.

The hoist hadn't been moved in who knows how long. The previous owners had called the whole building that housed it "off limits." The key to it working was to get the giant spool of wire to unwind, and then hopefully wind back up. A motor lets out cable to allow the cage to lower and then the motor takes that cable back up around a giant spool to make the cage come back.

If the worst case happened, and the frayed cable were to break, there was one safety measure in place. The hoist has "dog ears," or giant metal half-moons with teeth all along them. The tension on the cable during descent or ascent keeps the teeth pulled back so the cage can glide along the shaft. The instant the cable goes slack, however, for example if the cable snaps, the dog ears clamp in like a bear trap, biting deeply enough into the wooden rails that run down the shaft to keep the cage from plummeting to the bottom of the pit. That's the theory, anyway.

The truth is those wooden guard rails are a hundred years old, at least. Dry-rotted in some places, missing altogether in others, and if Tip's memory is correct, there's a good chance that some of the old rails are so water-logged that in the event of an emergency the iron teeth would just slice right through them, like ice skates on the surface of a slushy pond. Even under the best of bad circumstances, going full speed there is little hope that these old rails would bear the weight of the metal cage, three grown adults and a slew of tools. In that case, we'd be in free fall. At least the end would be quick.

The day we were set to test the hoist by sending a three-hundred-pound ore bucket down to the 86-level (we didn't want to take any chances with humans before doing a little dry run), John Bowden pulled me aside to let me know how much this trip down to the water meant to Tip. Getting the water going was something Tip had dreamed of doing for many years. There had been a lot of false starts, broken promises, and frustration during that time. At one point, he'd even purchased a new replacement pump with his own money, only to have the plans to install it scrapped. Tip might have been tight-lipped about it, but he was beginning to fear that the water trapped in the mountain would remain trapped forever. Now that he was measuring his life in months if not weeks, this hastily formed "water crew" was likely his last best chance to get the pump installed and see the water flow again. I can't tell you that it was the hope of reaching that water again, of freeing it, that was keeping Tip alive. But I can tell you this, as much as I wanted that water myself, as much as I wanted it for Cerro Gordo, I wanted it for Tip even more. I wanted that water to be part of his legacy.

I didn't know John Bowden well at the time, so I didn't know how much of the story could be true. But it was true enough. When Tip passed away some months later, his friends made a grave marker out of a silver bucket, a precious replica of the one so much depends on. On the outside, they listed all the things he had wanted to do before he "kicked it." At the top of the list was getting the water going again at Cerro Gordo.

When it came time to venture to the 700-level, the decision about the final two members of the inaugural three-man crew (the cage could fit only three, very uncomfortably at that) was hotly debated. I own the mine, so naturally I was in. John Bowden bowed out due to lung issues and concerns over the oxygen levels at that depth. Cody had absolutely no interest in ever going under the earth. "It doesn't make sense and I want no part of it," he said. That left Tip, Craig, and Dave.

Tip, being the oldest of the bunch, the one who had for sure been down to the 700-level before, and the one donating the pump we were going to be using, was the obvious next choice.

From there, Tip chose Craig. He'd been watching Craig in much the same way he'd been watching me and saw that Craig was a doer, a guy who you just knew could, if necessary, MacGyver a fix for just about anything. And down at the 700-level, "anything" was a distinct possibility.

With that, the crew was set. Tip, Craig, and I would be the first to venture into the depths of the mine, while Dave stayed up top with Cody and John. It felt a bit like we were picking the astronauts to go to the moon. Except none of us were going to be heroes and we had no mission control to mitigate the danger. If something went wrong, very few people outside of our immediate circle would ever know. And fewer still would care.

To prepare, we gathered any and all tools we could think of that might be useful down in the hole. Craig, decked out in his insulated red-and-black Snap-on jacket, procured a Sawzall (which would prove invaluable), multiple foot-long bolts, a drill and drill bits, a harness (which would also prove invaluable), flashlights, and maybe a Coors Banquet or two. Tip wrapped himself in multiple jackets, a few beanies, and took a bucket with some hammers in it. Before stepping into the cage to complete the cargo that Cody would be lowering into the depths, I stuffed my pockets with hand warmers, a few headlamps for good measure, and a camera to capture the moment.

Nothing reminds you that you are dangling precariously from a thin metal rope like stepping onto a rickety old hoist cage. It groaned and shifted like a teeter-totter under our weight as we tried to space ourselves so we could balance it. Every little movement felt like the cage was trying to slip out from its cable and hurl itself to the bottom of the mine.

I should have been terrified. Part of me probably was. But as we rattled and bounced and ratcheted our way down deeper into the mine, an overwhelming sense of excitement overtook our unspoken fear.

Under the best of circumstances, it should have taken us about forty-five minutes for the cage to clatter its way down to the 700-

level. But these were far from the best of circumstances. We spent hours in that cage, repairing the damage of the last few decades on our way down. When we weren't working, we were mostly silent. Which leaves a lot of time to think. Occasionally there was small talk, but I think for the most part we were all thinking our own thoughts about the descent. Is this how fast it always goes? How would I jump out if I had to? What if something happened to Tip? What if he had an emergency?

"If something goes wrong," Tip said suddenly, breaking the silence. "Then leave me down there." I guess it was brave. It was not what I wanted to think about. Then, perhaps sensing the effect he'd had on the mood, he snapped us out of it. "Nobody's dying," he stated sternly from the back of the cage, no headlamp on, enjoying the still of the darkness.

"The 86!" I mouthed to myself as I recognized the first portal into the mine. The 86-level, originally referred to as the Buena Vista tunnel level, was tapped in 1865. It was the first level on Belshaw's descent down to tap into the Jefferson Chimney. My months studying those history books were coming alive. These mythical levels that I thought I'd never see were suddenly right in front of me. Everything felt more real. Everything felt more important.

I remember peering so far over the edge to get a glimpse at what was coming up at us that my hard hat got knocked off by a passing timber.

"Careful," Tip said calmly, a slight twinkle in his eyes that I hadn't seen since the first time we'd walked a wash together.

"Take care of my dogs!" Craig yelled up to Dave as the cage moved lower still. The light above us started to recede into a pinpoint and the cool air of the shaft enveloped us.

The trip down was indeed slow and dangerous, and impeded by hazards that made our long descent even longer. A couple of times, the cage got stuck in places where the guide rails were so warped they stopped us in our tracks. Craig, tethered to his harness like an astronaut on a spacewalk, climbed out of the cage, dangled from it with nothing except several hundred feet of pitch-black nothing beneath him, and fixed each problem, drilling new bolts into the old wood to hold them just far enough back to let us pass. Even 150 years after they were put in, the beams still gave the drill bit a fight. The sawdust smelled the same as new wood. Old growth timber. That was a relief.

Against all odds we eventually did make it safely down there. The 700-level. Stepping out of the cage it struck me just how long it had been since any human being had stood here. The last man who stood where I'm standing would probably barely recognize the world above. But he'd know this place. It hasn't changed.

Tip was not given to such sentimental thoughts, nor was he one for reflecting on the historical significance of our achievement, at least not in words. He had more practical objectives in mind and so he brusquely pushed past us; strode directly over to the old piston pump, layered with caked-on oil and dirt; inspected it; and began plotting exactly what we needed to do to get it up and running. Craig joined him and began surgically poking and prodding the electricals.

I, who have no such skills, was redundant, and so I decided to go exploring, spelunking deeper into the horizontal tunnel.

That's when I found it. I felt it long before I saw it, felt that quickening in my core, felt it on my skin even though I was bundled up against the bitter cold in the mine. Any man, when he's thirsty enough, becomes a human divining rod. I pushed forward a few more yards, over a small collapse, and the beam of my flashlight suddenly reflected back at me from the placid surface of a pool of water, fifteen feet long, ten feet across, and at least six feet deep.

"There it is," I said to myself. "Take it."

But I wasn't Mulholland, poaching somebody else's water. This water was mine, morally and legally. Under the byzantine water laws of the State of California I had the literal legal claim to it and the documents to prove it.

Silver. Zinc. Of all the precious commodities that have been wrested from this hole in the ground, none have ever been as precious as the water from that small pool. You can live without silver, you can live without zinc. But water is life.

I'd been in many mines by that point and never encountered water. The existence of it is very strange in a dry mine shaft. The mines around Cerro Gordo are known for preserving artifacts so well because there is almost no moisture. Now, right in front of me, were thousands of gallons of water, seven hundred feet below the earth. The water seeped in through the walls of the shaft in this particular level only. At some point the miners realized enough of the water was dripping down that they could pool it. So they dug a basin out of the rock, hacked out a small V-shaped trace to capture and funnel more of the water that seeped down the mine walls, and suddenly in this dark and dry place there was an in-ground swimming pool.

I wonder what the miners must have felt when they first discovered this. I know what I felt.

To me, it felt like coming upon the heart of Cerro Gordo.

Back at the pump, Tip and Craig were talking excitedly. To everyone's surprise, it seemed the power was going to work. The pump replacement looked relatively straightforward. We all stood there, taking it all in. We had survived the trip down. We had seen the mythical water in the rock.

We had a plan. The future of Cerro Gordo was looking brighter than it had in a very long time.

And we all seemed to realize that around the same time.

After we did a bit of exploring and note-taking on next steps, we shuffled back into the hoist. The trip back up was a lot more chatty than the trip down had been. We were firing off new ideas. Even Tip had a joke or two to share as we climbed out of the depths of the earth.

As I was going back up, I felt as though the future of the town was in my own hands. We had found water. But more than anything, I was overcome by a profound sense of camaraderie.

Belonging. True community. It was something I had never experienced.

I've spent the majority of my adult life living in big cities. New York City, Los Angeles, Austin. All towns with millions of inhabitants. And I have always felt painfully alone in those places. Then I moved to Cerro Gordo. I packed up my truck and drove myself as far away from other humans as I had ever been in my life. I'd manufactured my own isolation. I'd leaned into loneliness. The only way it could have felt any more like living on an abandoned island was if I'd had to swim there. And yet, as I got to know the water crew, any vestige of that loneliness completely disappeared.

This is the thing about the desert compared to the city. In the city, you are thrust into relationships of convenience and inconvenience by virtue of proximity. You are stacked on top of each other, crammed together, jammed next to each other. On a daily basis, you have no choice but to deal with dozens, sometimes hundreds, of utter strangers. Your interactions are often stilted, ritualized, and, for the most part, transactional. You deal with them and they with you because you need something from one another, a cup of coffee, a mortgage, an extra foot of personal space in the line for the ATM. Little by little, perhaps before you even realize it, you come to resent these strangers, you come to view them as petty thieves stealing your time, your space, your energy, your parking spot, until eventually you withdraw and build a wall around yourself.

That doesn't happen in the desert. Here relationships develop by choice. They're like the pinyon pines that dot the hillsides. They are few but their roots are deep. This is as much a product of circumstance as it is constitution. Desert rats like the guys on the water crew want their space.

They enjoy their isolation. They don't like or trust lots of people—as individuals or as large groups like cities—because most people expect things to be given to them. Instead, they've chosen to live like little deserted islands themselves, in a place defined by scarcity, where there are countless things that you could always use more of but that you can never expect will just be given to you. In the desert, you have to work for your piece of the abundance to the extent it's there to be had. You have to be resilient and self-sufficient, knowledgeable and effective.

If you're not any or all of those things, folks in the desert have no time or energy for you. If you are those things, however, or if you show yourself to be someone who is trying to become all those things, then what you find is not a collection of hardened recluses but a community of the most welcoming, helpful people you will ever meet. You'll find a family, except better, because they don't come with all the baggage and they'll give you the shirt off their backs without holding it over your head.

Desert friends will drive three hours to pull your car out of the sand. They will come out to your place and help you clear a mouse infestation or a rattlesnake problem. They'll help you fix a fence, build a road, tear down a wall. In my case, they offered me machine parts and old wood to use; they rewired buildings on a moment's notice; they showed me what they were working on and shared what they cared about; they taught me how to walk the wash and helped me reach water.

Even more than that, the guys on the water crew have given me every piece of advice they could think of because they know better than I ever could exactly what I've gotten myself into out here. These guys have been building and operating establishments in the desert for decades. They've been through it. They know. Their generosity has made my hardest times easier. Their warnings have come true and saved me. And their belief that getting the water into town was possible has made me a believer that anything I want to do up here is possible.

Everyone who endeavors to tackle a huge, life-defining project, who intends to make a spectacle, needs a group of people in their life like the water crew. It is so easy to get lost inside a big dream. The obsession and focus required to bring something massive into existence can be so complete at times, you don't just lose your way, you can also lose yourself. You need someone who has been there before.

You need someone who can show you the way out and show you the way through. You need someone who sees what you see, but knows what you don't know.

That I'd found a crew of guys like this, out here in the middle of nowhere, who had my back, was one of the most profound realizations of my life. This dream I have for Cerro Gordo, it's not impossible. And it's not mine alone. I am not alone.

CHAPTER 7

NEED WATER

They call it Death Valley for a reason. On average, three or four people die each year in Death Valley National Park. The reasons range from car accidents to climbing falls to snakebites, but by far the most painful and most tragic, and the one that produces the most search and rescue calls, is an eager tourist with a taste for adventure.

The would-be adventurer wants to visit the desert. But not just any desert, the hottest and most notorious desert in America. And they don't just want to visit it or drive through it, they want to explore a part of that desert that nobody has been to before. So they rent a van or an SUV and they head out, letting nobody know where they're going or that they're going somewhere that nobody should go. They turn off the main road onto a dirt road and drive. They're looking for some famous ruin, some secret spot they read about online. A secluded hot spring or an old cabin. The directions aren't precise, but that's part of the thrill.

They think they found the next dirt road to go down, except it's not a road. It's just the gravelly portion of a wash that is about to turn sandy and get deep very quickly. Inevitably, they get stuck. The driver hammers the accelerator, but all that does is sink the van deeper into the sand. The passenger gets out and tries to push while the driver guns it again. But nothing. Now panic starts to set in. The driver jumps out and starts trying to dig out around the buried tires. They check their phone. No signal. Their heart rate spikes, they start to sweat, they get very thirsty. The driver jumps back in and hits the gas. It didn't work the last time and it won't work the thirty next tries, in fact, it's only digging them in deeper. Burning gas, killing battery.

They are officially stranded. Blame is passed around. Foolish plans suggested. Panic devolves into desperation as everyone in the vehicle begins to wrestle with a newfound appreciation for why Death Valley is named what it is.

That name has been around since as long ago as 1850, when a group of pioneers was lost in the valley, assuming it would be where they'd die. Like the famous Donner Party two hundred miles to the north a few years earlier, they'd been stuck in the valley for nearly eight weeks, at the mercy of equally cruel elements. Some of the party had died, and they'd resorted to eating their mules and oxen to survive, drinking the blood to quench their thirst, making the heinous calculation about a final descent into barbarity. Finally ditching their wagons and hiking out of the mountain ranges, a woman in the group turned and said, "Goodbye, death valley." A name that has stuck around for more than a century, for good reason.

The National Park Service advises on their website, under the SAFETY heading on the Death Valley page: "Stay on paved roads in summer. If your car breaks down, stay with it until help comes." That, however, goes against the desire to act. To do SOMETHING. So usually the guy leaves his partner, half out of anxiety from doing nothing and half out of the ingrained expectation of being the hero who rescues the damsel in distress.

This is when he learns that life isn't a fairy tale. That those minutes traveled by car translate to hours on foot. This is when he finds out there is nowhere and nobody to walk to and that his tiny moving body is invisible to planes who may be flying overhead.

Exhaustion sets in. Along with dehydration. Realizing his mistake, he can turn back to the vehicle and his hopeful partner, and deal with the bleakness that will descend on both of them with nightfall. Or he can continue toward whatever made-up destination he has in mind. Either way, he'll die. Most often, the person who stayed with the vehicle will live.

That was the possible fate in store for a lone traveler on a warm August day in Death Valley before being lucky enough to be spotted by three guys in a Jeep who thought they were going on their own desert adventure that day, but were very happy to be able to help out. We never got around to asking the stranded man his name, so I'll call him Roy. I wonder if Roy knew the razor's edge he walked on, what kind of gamble he had taken. I doubt it. The human impulse is to see ourselves as smarter and stronger than the world. The look in Roy's eyes told me he didn't know, but that he was learning, quickly. Unfortunately, this is one of those lessons that sometimes has to be learned from experience. Fortunately, his was an experience he was able to survive.

His eyes were wide and wild, full of panic and desperation. He could barely force his thirst-swollen tongue and parched mouth to spit out the only two words that could save him.

"Help me."

I could see by looking at him that he didn't belong here. The words on his hat—the name of some law firm—were all the evidence I needed to know that this man had made a terribly wrong turn somewhere along the line. This is not the time of day to be walking the desert. The only plants still living this time of year have curled inward for the day. Any living creatures are hiding in the deep cracks in the soil.

This is hiding time in the desert. A time for shade. Not a time to be walking down a washed-out asphalt road, many miles from any source of shade or cell service.

His eyes pleaded with us in a way his words could not.

"My wife. My kid. We're stuck," he managed to choke out, pointing vaguely into the distance. Somewhere, beyond the endless field of Joshua trees, in the shadow of the Inyo Mountain range, his wife and kids were trapped in a van with dwindling water.

Meeting Roy was not on my agenda that day. I had no intention of even going into Death Valley. I had started my day some eight thousand feet above this deadly desert, where the temperature had been a cool seventy-five degrees, and the wind blew nicely. It had been a perfect day, tending to different tasks that are always in need of doing in an abandoned town with dozens of buildings. A pig in mud I was, happily slopping tar on the museum roof when I heard a dual-sport motorbike ripping up our road far too quickly. I could tell by the speed and the clapped-out sound of the engine that the man on top of the 1,100cc beast was Tim. Or "Tim Australia" as he is saved in my phone.

Growing up in Australia, Tim got into competitive downhill mountain bike riding at an early age. He apparently won all sorts of contests until some injury threw him off the sport. That's when he jumped on the back of a dirt bike and never looked back. Whether it was his Australian genes or his injury, it seems that his amygdala was nonexistent. He didn't just accept danger, he thrived in it.

Tim and I had started going on more and more adventures since he drove up to Cerro Gordo to "check out the new owner." I bought my first dirt bike, a red Honda CRF250, and we started riding to go see things. We'd take long trips into Death Valley to go see petroglyphs from three thousand years ago. We'd take single-track trails on the side of cliffs to get to untouched mines.

If I ever wanted an adventure, Tim always had a few in mind.

On the day we encountered Roy, Tim wanted to go to a mine deep in Death Valley that promised to have multiple levels, ore carts, dynamite, and more. By this point, our relationship had gotten to the platonic version of second base and Tim was telling me about all the mines he went to (and I was doing the same). Hearing what might be in store was all I needed to peel me away from weatherproofing against snow that wouldn't come for another six months.

Scotty, our town manager at the time, decided to come along, too. And given that there was going to be three of us, along with gear, Scotty's Jeep was the only vehicle that would work.

The bikes would have to stay at home that day.

We loaded up a few hundred feet of climbing rope, our harnesses, extra water, granola bars, our inReach GPS, and told the lone remaining worker in town, Richard, where we were going and to look after the town.

It was late in the day to start an adventure. That was especially true in this case because it would take two hours just to get to the mine Tim was telling us about. Most of that time off the main highway and up Saline Valley Road, a very unforgiving, unmaintained track of dirt and broken asphalt that twisted and rose and fell with the mountains and then traced a large wash that took you well outside of cell phone reception into the interior of the valley. If we got stuck or stranded out there, we would be there for the night.

About an hour into the dead zone, halfway down Saline Valley Road, we spotted Roy.

"Is that a dude?"

"Out here? It can't be."

"No dude, I think that's a dude!" Scotty exclaimed excitedly.

"Should we pick him up?"

"We have to pick him up."

"See what he wants."

"What if he kills us?"

"He could have a gun!"

"WE could have a gun."

The three of us were still bickering when we finally got close enough to Roy to see he was not simply a dude but a pitiable human in a great deal of distress. More than just sympathetic, he looked out of place, like he had dressed for the beach, and somehow been teleported to the surface of Mars.

As gingerly as we could, we got Roy into the back of Scotty's Jeep and started down the rutted desert track toward his van and the suffering woman and child he had abandoned with it. There was not a single bump on that several-mile drive that did not say: This is a bad way to go. You should not be here. Roy and his family had ignored every one of these warnings. I have no idea what possessed him to keep going. The road—if you could call it that—was so bad that one jounce violently snapped off a dancing hula figurine on our dash. The road was shrieking, STOP. TURN AROUND. THIS IS NOT A GOOD IDEA. And yet this man kept right on going.

As one does. As one does.

The three of us had a full conversation through silent glances in the rearview mirror, out of Roy's line of sight, while he downed a couple bottles of water and directed us to where his vehicle was stuck and his family was waiting.

How did he even make it back this far?

If we hadn't found him, he'd totally be dead.

Man, I hope his wife and kid are OK.

You can say a lot with your eyes when the stakes are this high.

"Thank you, thank you," Roy kept saying under his breath, in between gulps of water.

As we got closer to Roy's vehicle, his mood began to swing wildly. We could see it in his eyes and the way his body would periodically jerk up and then slump back into the seat. He was elated that he was safe and able to bring help to his young family. He was terrified that it had been eight hours since he'd left his wife and baby in a car in the middle of Death Valley. The thought of what might be waiting . . .

Around the bend of a large rock outcropping the vehicle came into view for the first time. It was a Sprinter van . . . of course. Over the last dozen years or so, as the whole ecotourism craze has taken hold among the affluent denizens of leafy suburbs, Mercedes Sprinter vans have become the go-to exploration vehicles for the rich and clueless. They're comfortable, easily modifiable, and surprisingly affordable right off the showroom floor, less than $50,000, which only encourages people with money to burn to deck them out with tens of thousands of dollars in upgrades. Fold out bedding, portable kitchen off the tailgate, tow package and light bars, auxiliary fuel tank, there is almost no end to how you can trick out a Sprinter van. In the most capable hands, a Sprinter rigged like an off-road vehicle can get you to and from reasonably inhospitable rugged areas in extremely comfortable fashion. In less experienced hands, they can get someone into much worse trouble than they could normally get into with a less capable vehicle. In cases like that, in cases like Roy's, the vans are a liability.

The position of the van told the whole story. Roy had followed a road that had turned into a wash, which had dissolved into plain desert. When any semblance of a followable path disappeared, Roy had realized his prospects of going any farther were slim, so he decided to turn around. It's not the fall that kills you, they say, and here it was the same—it was the turning around that did Roy in. He had left the partially packed-down dirt and put his tires onto virgin sand. At some point in his three- or four-point turn, it all came to a very sudden stop. More gas, more tries only succeeded in sinking all the tires into the sand.

His wife burst out of the van when she saw Roy climb from our backseat. "Oh, thank you!" she said as she rushed to hug her exhausted, and now relieved, husband. Their child smiling in her arms.

As is almost always the case with these vehicle rescues in Death Valley, getting them unstuck was far less eventful than the twists and turns that landed them there. Tim asked if I'd be willing to sacrifice one of my climbing ropes since we didn't have anything else. Doubling the rope and attaching one end to the back wheel well of the

Sprinter and the other to Scotty's front bumper, we had our method. Tim jumped in the Sprinter and instructed Scotty to back up at a forty-five-degree angle. A bit of extra pull in the right direction and the tires came jumping out of their holes.

Desert physics at its finest.

As we said our goodbyes, I saw a man who had learned the power of the desert, a man who knew what it was like to stare your own death in the face. I could not judge him too harshly. I knew that look, I knew that feeling.

Twelve months earlier, I'd had the exact look in my eyes as I curled up under a large rock, long past the point of dehydration, waiting for Tim to find me. It's not a proud tale of how I found myself there, but it's an important one, because I knew better and still I found myself face up on the dirt, staring at the prospect of the same kind of miserable death that Roy was only a few hours away from facing when we found him. The only difference was, I had told someone where I was going ahead of time. And that very well could have saved my life.

My goal that particular day was to hike the entirety of the Salt Tram—a long-defunct tramway set up in 1911 to transport salt out of Saline Valley (in Death Valley) up and over into Owens Valley to the railroad near Keeler that was originally constructed for Cerro Gordo. The tramway stretches fourteen miles over some of the most inhospitable terrain in the entire United States. It starts in the barren flats of Saline Valley, at one thousand feet above sea level, where the temperatures regularly break 120 degrees in the summer and where, in 2021, it reached 130 degrees Fahrenheit to become the hottest place on the planet. From the valley floor, the tramway climbs the eastern face of the Inyo Mountains, over a dozen or so small valleys, over treeless hillsides covered in loose shale, up and down, up and down, until it reaches the summit station at 8,500 feet.

It was going to be a brutal hike, but I had been eager to try it ever since I had met a guy early on in my time at Cerro Gordo who made it his life's mission to walk down the Salt Tram. To him, every one of the support stations was a feat of engineering. Something to be studied. Marveled at. Enjoyed. The passion with which he talked about the Salt Tram led me down a rabbit hole of research, and the more I read, the more I realized he was right. The Salt Tram may be one of the most impressive things constructed in the early 1900s. Much like old Burro Schmidt, who was busy hammering away one hundred miles south, two brothers grew tired of bringing their salt around a pass to get it into Owens Valley where it could be sold and shipped. Instead, they looked at the mountain range blocking their way and said THERE, we will go straight over the top of that range.

At the time, salt was a hot commodity. They first started harvesting salt in Saline Valley around 1903. The salt left behind by the water in the area was 99 percent pure and known as the finest in the country. Demand was high, but the cost of shipping it around the pass was too much. It took them two days of shipping to go what would be twelve miles over the mountains.

So starting in 1911, they spent three years and $750,000 dollars constructing the Salt Tram. The equivalent of over $20 million today. The tram required one million board feet of lumber and over six hundred tons of iron. All of which had to be transported on hillsides with grades up to 25 percent. In some places, the vertical angle from structure to structure could be as much as 40. They ran over fifty miles of metal cable that would end up supporting dozens of metal buckets that carried salt, supplies, and workers—sometimes all at the same time. Along the way, men and mules died to make this dream a reality. When the tramway was finished, it was the largest, most elaborate, and steepest tram in the world.

My hike directly below the Salt Tram's cable path, and those forty-degree declines, started one fateful June morning. A morning that just so happened to be in the middle of the hottest heat wave the infamous Death Valley had ever experienced. Temperatures that day were anticipated to reach 130 degrees in the valley floor. There was even talk that it could reach the hottest recorded temperature in history . . . a fine day for a hike.

A more experienced hiker out here would probably have taken the time to calculate the debilitating effects of the heat that was expected that day and a wiser man would probably have postponed the trip until a cooler day. But I thought I had a good safety plan in place, including staying in touch with Tim via Garmin inReach, which connects to satellites, allowing me to maintain communication even far out of cell phone range. Tim and I even set up a tracking link so Tim's wife, Janelle, could follow my progress along the trail from her computer. (Yes. This madman is married.) The plan was that Tim would meet me at the end of the path for pickup.

I was to depart around six or seven in the morning, about an hour after sunrise, and planned on meeting Tim around twelve hours later on the valley floor. If you viewed the trip only in terms of the miles I needed to cover, twelve hours seemed to be plenty of time. Just to be on the safe side Tim would bring extra water and Gatorades and I packed one and a half gallons of water in my pack. A bit more than I'd typically bring, but given the heat, it seemed very reasonable.

Beyond Tim, I told a few of the people in town of my adventure and shared with them my Garmin link where they could also follow along.

It seemed like a good plan, and the morning of the adventure started as beautifully as it could. Even with the heat wave, it was chilly waking up, so as I packed up my red Honda 250 to ride over to the summit station, I threw on a winter windbreaker and some insulated gloves. Only a few hours later such a decision would feel comically overdone.

The ride over to the summit station is possibly the most beautiful ride in the area. Starting at Cerro Gordo, you turn up the grade to an off-camber shale road. The road snakes around the far corner of the mountain range and suddenly you have the entirety of Owens Valley in your view. Down to your left you see the outline of what was once Owens Lake with its pastel palette of different colors, both man-made and natural. The Sierras that time of morning have a pink hue behind them and are typically covered in purple reflection. Down the valley you can see Owens River before it is redirected. An oasis in the desert. The trees and shrubbery follow the snaking river with the occasional cow herd or pack of wild horses.

Once you get a few miles from Cerro Gordo, the terrain becomes much more heavily wooded. It's the only place I've seen mule deer around here. Travel a bit farther and you get to Mexican Spring, which was one of the two springs those enterprising miners tapped in the 1800s to temporarily slake the thirst of the young town. Like the silver in the hills, this bounty from nature would quickly be sucked dry, though the unusual proliferation of new-growth trees and animal tracks near the spring seemed to hint that maybe, just maybe, the spring might be preparing to someday flow again.

Finally, after dirt biking through meadows, forests, and deserts, you make your first glimpse of the summit station. Long, wooden, and dominating the top of the ridgeline. I stopped my bike and just stared. The entire structure, even from a mile away, appears massive. I could tell even from there that the timbers must have been the width of trees. The contrast of the front of it looking into Saline Valley and the back of it looking into Owens Valley.

The remote location and size of the summit station still doesn't make sense to me. It just seems an impossible task to build such a feature in such a place. But after seeing some of the stations farther down the line, that station seems to be a walk in the park to build.

I arrived at the station when the pinks and purples were still streaking the sky over Death Valley, a stark contrast to the bone-colored salt flats below. Walking out to the end of the wooden planks, the valley floor looked as if it was a million miles away. It was like looking at the arid, etched plain from an airplane window. It didn't seem real.

I shot a text to Tim, letting him know I was starting my descent, and started scrambling down the shale, excited to see what few had seen in the past hundred years.

The first two stations are relatively easy to get to. The grade isn't too bad, the top of the summit is still in view, and you haven't quite got a full picture of all the torture ahead.

The awe of each station made any hesitations I had dissolve away. Any visible trails between them were long gone, so any clues on how they went about building these forty-foot-tall wooden towers on the side of cliffs have long since disappeared. The wood was the golden-brown hue that only timbers baked in this desert kiln for a century get. The steel cable was still hanging, a testament to the men who built the tram.

Riders on the tramway would have experienced something few else had, a commanding view of the world from on high. The Wright brothers had completed the first airplane flight only a few years prior. The world's first commercial flight wouldn't happen for another few years after the tramway was finished. To those who were able to ride the tramway, swinging thousands of feet above the ground, it must have felt like being an eagle or a condor. To ride over such steep cliffs, swaying in a small steel bucket, looking down at the deep wash below was something of a fairy tale. A perspective we take for granted these days, but would have been revolutionary in its time.

Its time, of course, is long past. Soon enough, even the memory of it will be gone.

Wood doesn't last forever, so I can't imagine these towers still existing in another hundred years. If only a handful of people do the whole hike each year, that means only a few hundred people may ever see the Salt Tram in all its faded grandeur. I felt like I was in rarefied air. The first quarter of the hike I was marveling at all that was around me. Trips like that help remind me what is possible. That beauty of possibility. Of trying daring things.

Humans are naturally drawn to massive things other humans have done in the past. Think about the most visited sites in the world—Colosseum, Parthenon, Pyramids, Taj Mahal, Eiffel Tower, Statue of Liberty, Great Wall of China. People visit these things for different reasons, but I think a main one is to be reminded what our species can do if we put our minds to it. It helps put whatever we're struggling with in perspective. For me, it inspires me to dream bigger. Reach even further. It connects me with the past and leaves me in a state of awe of what others have done before me.

And that feeling only seems to exist looking at physical structures, or nature. I've never looked at an app on my phone screen and felt the same way. Even though that app may have taken every bit as much ingenuity and dedication to create, in a hundred years or a thousand, will anyone look at our digital creations and experience the same sense of awe I felt in the presence of this engineering marvel? I can't imagine so.

Sometime after my second Clif bar and the fourth tower, the full picture of the path in front of me came into focus. It wasn't just one canyon I would be walking down. It was a series of canyons, each with a sharp incline, then decline, that lined the route leading to the valley floor below. I counted at least six such peaks and valleys I would have to walk up, over, and down on my trek.

My blood sugar and hydration levels were still high enough at that point that the adventure in front of me felt just like that—an adventure.

As I continued to slip and slide down the shale, it was easier to imagine aliens existing than how they placed some of the stations. Steep cliffs, on over forty-degree slopes, made of loose rock, miles and miles from any road and many more miles from any wood supplier.

Bewilderment. That's the best word to describe the Salt Tram and all its aging towers. For the first few hours of the hike, I could not get it out of my head how difficult the men who built the tramway must have had it. Seeing feats like that gives perspective. Reminds you what is possible. Puts your own problems in scale. I sat down at one of the towers and drank my second water bottle of the day, proud of myself for getting out and doing these explorations.

Of course, such contemplations are only possible when your base security is set. As they say, leisure is the mother of philosophy. About halfway through the hike, I found myself doing less navel-gazing and more practical thinking as the terrain got more and more challenging and my water supply dwindled.

Terminal 12 is the most intact and most famous tramway stop along the Salt Tram, though few of those who spoke of it had ever seen it with their own eyes. By sometime around high noon, I was standing at its base. Like everything else in the desert, the harder it is to get to, the fewer people have been there, and the more things from the past that remain.

This terminal had been the first thing my visitor in town told me about once we launched into our conversation about his lifelong mission to see all the stations. Tip was the only other guy I had ever met who had hiked the length of the trail, and Terminal 12 was the thing he remembered most about the whole trek. It was a piece of the past frozen in place.

All the buckets that once hauled salt are still dangling in the air. Pickaxes, some dull, others sharpened, are still neatly arranged on shelves within the station. There are full buckets of grease, still waiting to be slathered over the wheels. Ancient tin pots with chipped white enamel and rust holes sit around a faint fire ring. There are even torn up blue jeans, hidden under the base of the terminal, as if someone was one day going to change back into them. It was like one day everyone packed up, and never came back.

Looking at the chairs, tables, and hammers left behind inside the old tram tower, I thought about all the items we produce and insert into our lives with such care, and how they will far outlive us and whatever purposes we use them for.

Everything about the building tells a piece of the story of the people who used to be there. Each item is a puzzle piece. And my mind struggled to fit the jigsaw together. I wish I had longer there to try to imagine what that space looked like when it was operational. Who was the last person there?

Why did they leave? What were their hopes and dreams?

As I was exploring around the terminal, I came across another sobering reminder. A logbook. Placed there in who-knows-when, the water-warped journal had entries from each of the past decades, dating back to the first days of the last quarter of the twentieth century. Once or twice a year, sometimes less frequently, a traveler would scribble their name, date of exploration, and a brief note about whatever was going on. Excited to join the short list of intrepid explorers who'd make the trek here, I flipped to the most recent entry and searched for a pen.

There, scrawled in thin ink, was the name of a traveler who wrote that he had come up from the Saline Valley side. Along with that piece of information he wrote, "used 200 ft of rope to get past the falls."

"Why would they need two hundred feet of rope?"

My mind trailed off. But I knew the answer, and I knew I did not have any rope with me.

My suspicions were confirmed less than an hour later as I made my way down increasingly steep and tall dry waterfalls. I was walking down a wash. But not the wide, rocky washes that Tip and I typically explored. This was a narrow canyon runoff, carved by millions of years of water. It was only about ten feet wide. The sides of it had been rubbed smooth over time and were anywhere between fifty and sixty feet tall. Running my hands along the sides felt like the sides of a swimming pool. I could imagine the floods ripping through here when the summer monsoons came.

Every few hundred yards in the ravine there was a small dry waterfall. The first three feet or so were easy to slide down, bringing back memories of being a child on the playground, laughing as I hurtled down the slides with my backpack, though now my backpack was full of increasingly diminishing amounts of water and food. Each slide was a commitment toward a path. Sliding down smooth rock is easy. Climbing back up smooth rock is not. If I were to get to a waterfall needing rope—say, two hundred feet of rope—there may be no way down, nor a way back up. Cliffed out.

A raven started circling me around that point. The insinuation felt rather rude given the circumstances, but I was somewhat relieved to have some company, no matter its species.

As I continued to slip and slide down dry waterfalls, I eventually came to a slightly larger one—ten feet tall.

Readjusting my backpack for the larger slide, I put my legs in front of me and started sliding on my butt—like I had done a dozen or so times by that point.

But as I was sliding down, the tiniest little branch made its existence known, catching on the bottom of my backpack and turning me to my side, landing me on my shoulder. My fall was broken by the side of my backpack. The area where I had both my water bottles . . . and my inReach.

"Fuck" is all I could think as I felt water running down my leg. My last two remaining water bottles had smashed on impact. I felt a sense of dread as their contents spilled onto the ground and were greedily sucked up by the small pockets of sand that accumulated in the cracks in the rock.

Losing those two precious bottles of water, especially at the stage I was at in the hike, could prove deadly. I had been consuming water at a much quicker pace than I had anticipated as the temperatures were already over one hundred degrees in the wash. Unsure of exactly how far I had left to go, I decided to check my inReach to get a rough mileage.

"Device is damaged, please contact the manufacturer."

No.

No.

No.

I shut down and restarted my device, very much in the denial stage of grief. After a few minutes of frantically pressing buttons and hoping for the best, I knew for certain I was screwed. The device was broken from the collision with the rock and was refusing to send or receive texts, or tell me my exact distance to the bottom.

With no other option, I decided to stay the course, continuing down the path that should lead me to where Tim was planning on picking me up.

By that point I was taking small, delicate steps. The steep downhill shale had shredded my muscles, plus at this point the lack of water was starting to really make things difficult. They say by the time you're a little thirsty, you are moderately dehydrated. I felt like I was flirting with what some medical providers would deem "terminal dehydration." Or, the end of the line. My muscles were spasming. I was having mini blackouts where my vision would fade inward and eventually fade to all black.

The plan, if this unfortunate situation were to occur, was that Tim would hike up some fluids from the bottom. By now I was within a mile or so of the bottom. So close. But then I remembered that Christopher McCandless had been not too much farther from a ranger's cabin that could have been his salvation when he perished in the Alaskan wilderness. A mile might as well be a million when you're alone. And I was alone. My messages were not going through to let Tim know of the situation.

Another lesson you learn in the desert is that no matter how bad things are, they can always get worse. You can make them worse—in fact, that's the vicious cycle that kills you. Delirious, desperate, exhausted, you come to a choice and you make the wrong one.

I stumbled forward to encounter what I had long dreaded. A sixty-foot waterfall made of smooth rock. No jagged edges to even rock climb down. My worst fears about that cryptic message in the logbook mentioning two hundred feet of rope were right there in front of me, etched in stone.

My face was vibrating with heat. I could feel my pulse in my cheeks, in my forehead, everywhere. My tongue was swollen and the slimy feeling in my mouth had been replaced with just dryness. My blackouts were getting more frequent and I knew I had to somehow cool my core temperature, and quickly. Given that I was in a dry riverbed with no trees, the only sanctuary I could find was a large rock, which in the afternoon sun afforded a thin sliver of shade. If I contorted my body and shimmied myself just right, I could get maybe half of my body into the shade.

As I lay down under the rock, I thought again of McCandless, who has inspired so many to love the outdoors and is simultaneously derided by most naturalists as a reckless amateur.

I identify deeply with McCandless's urge to explore, to live. Inside all of us is this thirst for something more. A life less ordinary. A call to return to nature, to surrender to the fact that nature doesn't care about your plans. Not McCandless's. Not mine. Not yours. Your ego and its grand ambitions are no match for the cruel majesty of nature. Especially in a location as dangerous as Death Valley during a heat wave. As I lay there, dehydrated, disoriented, and on the brink of disaster, I started bargaining with nature herself, vowing to her that I would be more respectful and cautious the next time we met if she'd just permit me to survive this time.

My supplications were interrupted by a voice calling out in the wilderness. That voice had an unmistakably Aussie accent.

"BREENNNNTTTTT!"

Tim was near enough for me to hear his voice bouncing off the canyon walls. I snapped out of my stupor. I couldn't pinpoint where the sound was coming from, couldn't see him from my spot beside the rock, and so, mustering all the remaining strength I had, I climbed my way back to the edge of the cliff. He let out a few more yells, but the echoes of the canyon walls played tricks on me. I could not tell how close they were or whether they were coming closer or fading farther away. I yelled back at the top of my lungs. I waited. And waited. Only to have silence return.

I felt defeated. Help, water, Gatorade, were all so close but still too far away to reach me. Now, a new level of fear bordering on panic began to set in. I began to imagine all kinds of horrible possibilities. What if Tim had gotten hurt? What if he wasn't calling out because he was ready to help me, but was instead crying out because he needed my help? The wash below the waterfall was extremely steep and filled with boulders the size of golf carts. Images of Tim getting crushed by a loose rockslide while coming to bring me water entered my head.

I summoned the last bit of strength I had. In fact, I summoned strength I didn't know I had. It's a peculiarity of human nature that, when faced with an essential struggle, we tap our last reserves of strength to save ourselves. But dig even deeper, into some mysterious and occult part of ourselves, we find an extra measure of will to save someone else.

I suppose that, as much as anything, is what pushed me forward that last mile. I scoured the waterfall. The side I was on was worn smooth, and dropped sixty feet onto a pile of jagged rocks. I'd never make it down that. Looking more closely, I could see that here and there were branches from the few spindly trees that had managed to not only survive the relentless heat of the desert but also escape being washed away in the periodic extreme desert floods that are the stuff of legend around here. I figured if I played it just right, I could use those branches to pull myself to a spot along the waterfall where there was a perilously narrow space not much wider than my boot. I could fox-foot my way along that narrow path like a tightrope walker and make it to the far side of the falls, where there were rocks and boulders big enough for me to climb down to the bottom.

Weighing my options, it seemed that was the only way to go. I'd read an article not too long before about a guy who fell thirty feet on a dry waterfall. Rescue crews found him sometime after his death, not knowing for certain if he had died on impact or was severely injured and waited days and days before his inevitable demise.

Trying my best to not black out from dehydration, I slowly inched my way along the six-inch path.

Toe by toe I would look down and see the rocks waiting for me below. Hearing Tim had given me a second wind. Not hearing him had given me a sense of urgency. I made a promise that neither of us were going to die there.

After about an hour getting across the waterfall, I began making my way down the boulders in the wash. I still hadn't heard from Tim and was still concerned he might be pinned under a rock ahead. I thought of the newspaper headlines that would accompany such a foolish errand. The conversations I'd have with his family members. The remorse I'd feel for the rest of my life if things did not turn out all right.

A few minutes later, I turned a corner and saw something that definitely wasn't a rock. It was man-made, dark, and sticking straight up in the air. My brain had a hard time deciphering what it was. Eventually, I determined the thing I was looking at was an umbrella. Underneath the umbrella, sitting in a chair drinking iced Gatorade, was Tim. Relief swept over me. The newspaper would have to find different stories for tomorrow's run.

"Well, there was no use in both of us dying" was the first thing Tim said to me when I finally made my way over. The wash had been too steep and Tim had started experiencing blackouts of his own in the heat, so he had built himself some shade and was waiting for me to hopefully emerge alive. If I hadn't walked out when I did, Tim would have hiked in once the sun went down to find me.

Or so he swore.

We eventually made our way back to Tim's truck, then back to Bishop. After a few days of air conditioning, Gatorades, and rest, my parched, swollen tongue shrank back down and I was relatively sane again. Sane, with a new appreciation for water that one gets only from desperate experience.

Even if I had planned better, nature still would have had veto power over me. A rockslide, a sudden flash flood, a rattlesnake could have ended my hike, and life, in an instant. I could have been Christopher McCandless. I could have been the hapless lawyer. Nature has a way of humbling us, reminding us of our place in the world. The desert doesn't care about your wealth, your nationality, your profession. A hurricane isn't impressed by your zip code or the car you drive. Those things are only permitted to exist at all because nature suffers them to.

If nature teaches us anything, it's humility in the presence of a power greater than ourselves.

And that's one of my favorite things about being in nature. Being reminded of our relative insignificance and dependence on her being.

CHAPTER 8

TOO MUCH WATER

The road to Cerro Gordo has never been good. There's a lot of reasons why. It's in the middle of nowhere. It's built where nature didn't want roads. It rises sharply from the desert floor, climbing nearly a mile in the eight miles it takes to reach town, and as bad as it is going up, it's worse coming down, a white-knuckle flume to hell. It's the kind of road you'd only turn off onto if you really had to, and even then, you'd think twice about it. Sometimes you could say it's even been left broken on purpose.

Built in a wash, the road can vanish in one of those gully washers that erupt over the mountain from time to time. One minute it's a road—sort of—and the next it's a raging river. Nature always gets the final say about who will stay and what will go.

Most of the time there's nowhere near enough water. Those days you're on your knees praying for rain. Then the rain comes, and there's so much of it you wonder why you ever needed it to begin with.

It's always been that way in this desert. Cycles of drought followed by savage floods. The pilgrim miners who hacked Cerro Gordo into existence found themselves battling the dual evils of drought and flood almost from the moment they arrived. There was a legendary flood in 1882 that took out the entire road and almost took out a miner, Max Skinner, who later described the flood as "a wall of water coming down the canyon."

The miners in the path of the flood barely escaped, managing to frantically drive their panicked horses and themselves onto a dry spot on the side of the hill before the flood reached them. If they had been a few dozen yards farther up the road, they wouldn't have made it.

There was another washout on August 9, 1901. Described by the *Inyo Independent* as a "terrific cloudburst," the flood waters were powerful enough not to just wash away the road but also to displace gigantic boulders that had lined it. It was a puzzlement to the mine owner who, according to the newspaper, spent the next several days "looking up the most feasible route for a pack trail, and wondering what has become of the great boulders that used to line the road." When he finally found an alternate route, there'd be two fewer pack animals using it. Two horses made the grave mistake of grazing in the wrong place when the deluge hit. "[T]he animals have not been located since," the paper lamented.

These days, I tend to think of the road as a kind of time bomb, albeit a semi-sentient one, that maliciously waits until the most inopportune time to detonate itself, so it can inflict the maximum amount of damage.

My first experience with the maddeningly mercurial nature of nature and the savagery of her floods came at one of the worst times imaginable. As they often do.

The storm, which caused all the flooding, was so bad it could be seen from space. The National Weather Service called it a "thousand-year storm." That's a term that gets tossed around a lot these days and I think it merits some explanation. It does not mean that you get one of these raging storms and the floods that follow it once in a millennium and then after that you're golden for another thousand years. What it means is that gauged against the historical record, in any given year, there's one chance in a thousand that a storm of that magnitude might hit. Now, if you're a gambler, those odds may not seem too bad. The problem is the historical record is not as reliable as it once was. A changing climate has made dry places drier and wet places wetter, and over the past couple decades one-hundred-year storms, five-hundred-year storms, and one-thousand-year storms have been stacked up like airplanes over the skies of LAX.

Nine months' worth of rain fell in three hours on August 5, 2022, across the 3.4 million acres of Death Valley. By the time the skies cleared, cars, houses, even people, had been scoured from the desert. A week after the flood, over a thousand people were still missing or stranded inside Death Valley National Park.

When a storm like that comes, you can't run for it. And it wasn't even forecasted to be that bad. Well, not until it was basically on top of us. Live by the odds, die by the odds.

The truth is, we'd had pretty good weather in the preceding weeks, and as a result, the road had been in less terrible shape than it had been in years and the hotel rebuilding had benefited from it. We had been able to haul truckloads of blocks and rebar and cement onto the site, two hundred tons of it, to be precise. Because none of the local contractors would agree to risk the eight-mile-long drive up the rocky road to Cerro Gordo, we ended up doing the work ourselves, and that meant mixing eighty yards of concrete, by hand, in a single day. It takes a lot of water to mix eighty yards of concrete. About two thousand gallons, in fact, and that, too, had to be hauled onto the site.

Next, we needed a water tank to store water for the future fire sprinkler system of the future hotel. I'll save you the math on how the engineers got to the number, but we needed forty thousand gallons, on-site, at all times, or we couldn't have a hotel. So after much searching, I managed to locate a tank that size. It was forty-seven feet long and twelve feet tall. In Fresno, CA.

The reason I'm not expanding more on the whole adventure is because it went remarkably smoothly. For seemingly the first time in my quest to rebuild, the plan went just as, well, planned.

One of the guys who helped with the project, a guy named Jax, even went as far as to say: "This time, everything has gone oddly smooth. I'm still waiting for something to drop. Everything has just gone *so* smooth, I can't believe it."

Oh, and would something drop. But by the middle of that week, I was feeling pretty proud of myself.

We had finished putting up the final blocks in the basement of the hotel and all that remained was for the mason to come and tie in the last bit of rebar, then we'd be able to move to framing the building because the basement would, at long last, be complete.

And therein lay the rub.

Thursday came and the mason was missing. Dozens of calls and texts were not returned. I sent someone in his town over to check his house. His truck was gone, and all that was left was a sinking feeling.

I'd heard that he'd done this before, taken a large draw on a contract, and then, with a bit of cash in his pocket, holed himself up in some cheap motel for days on end.

We scrambled to find a replacement. But there wasn't a deep pool of talent to draw from. There are only three masons in our entire county. Ours was busy debauching himself while the other two were plain busy, working on other people's projects.

I had established a tight deadline for each phase of the project and the deadline had come and gone. Make plans, and God laughs. So, apparently, does my mason.

And then came Sunday. The skies opened and my 99.9 percent chance of escaping the most savage storm I had ever seen in my life got washed away in the deluge, along with the road.

There is, woven deep into the most primitive part of our brain, a sense of awe and terror in the pour of a storm. Even as we became increasingly walled off from the immediate experience of nature's fury, protected by the thick, sturdy walls of our modern homes and our vaunted infrastructure, our storm drains and man-made barriers to disaster, there has always been a sense that at any moment, nature might overwhelm us, as indeed, more and more often now, it does. That unconscious recognition of how vulnerable we are to storms is deeply integrated into our collective id. We've even woven the language of storms into our daily discourse, perhaps pretending that if we turn them into clichés, we'll rob them of their power.

We'll "storm" out of a room, and then, if we're feeling generous, we'll let a feeling of peace and charity "wash over" us, or, if you're the sort who's less inclined to be forgiving, you might be "flooded" with rage.

By Monday morning, I was "flooded" with a whole host of emotions.

On the night the storms hit, I had been out running last-minute errands, in a desperate hope that I might finish at least some of the masonry work myself. I had careened from Lone Pine to Ridgecrest to Bakersfield searching for commercial masonry equipment I could rent or borrow. By the time I had made it to the turnoff for our road, rain was falling in sheets, falling faster than my windshield wipers could remove it. Behind me, the state highway was flooded. Then I got word from the top. A text from someone who had tried to come back down and failed. They'd made it less than two miles before they had to turn around. "The road's gone" the text read.

"There's no way up."

"Fuck."

I don't know how long I sat there, rain pounding on my roof. I couldn't see more than a foot or two in front of me through the curtain of rain on my windshield, and so I looked back instead, all the way back to 1868, when Mortimer Belshaw first built that original Yellow Grade Road to Cerro Gordo. It was Belshaw, in all his genius and hubris, who willed the hole in the ground at Cerro Gordo into national prominence as one of the most valuable silver mines in California. A miner by trade and by temperament, he was a man who believed that with enough dynamite and grit, he could make nature bend to his will. He had been drawn to the place after hearing whispers of high-quality ore in these mountains, and he managed to secure for himself a third of the ownership in the only mine in town. When he and his partner took some of the ore to San Francisco to be assayed and discovered that it was indeed as pure as he'd been told, he began planning a future for the town, made entirely in his image. Rocks and people both give way if you hammer them long and hard enough, and Belshaw set about mining the well-heeled California for financial backing. He managed to persuade Egbert Judson, who would later become president of the California Paper Company, that he had tapped into the next Comstock Lode. Soon enough, Judson bought in. In 1868, they incorporated as the Union Mining Company and set their sights on controlling the entire hill.

If the Union Mining Company was going to make a killing, however, it first had to get it out of the mountain. That was no problem for Belshaw. He was a miner. That's what he knew. Getting it off the mountain, so it could be shipped and sold, was a different matter altogether.

Belshaw was nothing if not a man of supreme confidence in his own abilities, and so, in the hottest part of the summer of 1868, he began carving out the eight-mile Yellow Grade Road, named after the yellow-tinged shale the road cut through.

It took Belshaw and his crews months to construct the road. Those obstacles too steep to go over and too difficult to blast through had to be gone around, and that meant that road took a winding, serpentine course up the mountain. Miners then used to joke that the road was only fit for a drunk, with all its lurching twists and turns. In the narrowest parts of the road, if two wagons were to meet, the smaller of them would have to be disassembled and let the larger one pass before going on their way. But it served its purpose. Because of that road, Cerro Gordo turned into a boomtown. Belshaw, who was born knowing how to get blood from a stone, made it a toll road and charged every man, wagon, and mule $0.25 to use the road—and he hit you both directions.

But there was one other major flaw with Belshaw's road. From time to time it just disappeared. Heavy rains would just wash the whole road away. The truth is that wasn't a bug. It was a feature. Belshaw had built the road literally right through the middle of a wash.

In a way, people are like water. Both follow the path of least resistance, and when you're trying to carve a road through the mountains, the easiest option is to follow where the water would naturally go, to use what nature has already partially carved for you over the centuries. So Belshaw followed the wash, dynamited out a few sections to make the trip a bit straighter, and added "fill" on top of the riverbed to allow wagons to pass. This worked most of the time, as the Inyo Mountains average less than twelve inches of rain for the entire year, but when a rain does happen, it would lead to crashed wagons and worse.

Belshaw's next move in controlling the town was to control the refinement of the ore coming out of not only his mines, but anyone else's in the area. Previously, small furnaces made of clay, known as vasos, were used to refine the galena coming out of the mountain. To accommodate the larger operation Belshaw had in mind, he invented an entirely new furnace, never before seen anywhere else in the mining world. His "water jacket furnace" could refine nine tons of ore per day (eighteen thousand pounds), whereas the vasos would do their best to refine a few hundred pounds. Soon, Belshaw's furnace was running twenty-four hours a day, producing nearly $60 million a year of silver and lead (adjusted for inflation). In addition to refining his own ore, Belshaw would charge to refine other miners' ore in the area. If a miner couldn't pay their bills, Belshaw would take their mining claim, further expanding his domination of the young mining town.

One competitor, the Owens Lake Silver-Lead Company, started mining so much ore that they no longer wanted to be beholden to Belshaw and his furnace charges. Instead, in 1869, they built a refinery of their own, down on the shoreline of Owens Lake. But they still had to use Belshaw's road to get the raw ore down. Since it wasn't refined, the raw ore was much heavier and more cumbersome to bring large quantities off the hill. As Belshaw saw the Owens Lake company taking their refining business elsewhere, he devised a plan to make their trip as difficult as possible. Belshaw stopped almost all maintenance on his road, but continued to collect his tolls to get up the hill.

His hope was that by making it so difficult to get the raw ore off the mountain, the Owens Lake Silver-Lead Company would eventually have to return to using his furnace. He didn't mind screwing over everyone else in the process. All parties eventually found themselves in court in 1872, where Belshaw's lawyer, a one-armed attorney named Pat Reddy, argued that "if it has not been for the owner of that trail practically there would have been no Cerro Gordo, or need of any road at all." He was the trailblazer, and to the trailblazer go the spoils.

The ruling went in his favor. The toll remained. And the experience did not improve.

Now, a hundred and fifty years later, more than a century after his death, Belshaw's road is still taking its toll. On me.

Road or no road, I was desperate to get back to Cerro Gordo. I threw the truck into gear and went to see for myself whether the road really was impassable.

When I got to the section called "the narrows" I could no longer deny the damage. Our fate was sealed. A road, by definition, leads from one place to another. What I was looking at led nowhere. What

I was looking at was a riverbed. One with three-foot ravines and boulders bigger than a person.

And water, so much water.

I got out of my car and straddled two boulders to watch the water flow. The stream had tiny specks of sand swirling in it; red specks, yellow specks, gray specks. A galaxy of small pieces of rock, flatted and smoothed by all the one-thousand-year-storms before this one, hitchhiking a ride to the bottom of the hill. Each piece, multiplied by millions, taking our road, my plans, with it. There was nothing I could do. The sand racing below me didn't care how angry I got. How did the sand get up there in the first place? Maybe it was finally going home. Nature was returning to what it always was. Before men discovered ore higher up. Before Belshaw decided to put a road right here.

The washed-away sand revealed things I'd never seen on the road before. On the exposed bedrock there were scrape marks from what I assume were wagons from back in the day. Higher up in the narrows I saw two drilled holes on either side and put together that they must have been for winching up wagons.

I wonder how Belshaw must have felt seeing the road come to life. He had moved to the town because he thought he could make it as big as his dreams, that the potential of the town was larger than anyone could imagine; anyone, that is, except himself. And went all-in. He built this road to make his dream come true and to make everyone else bend to it. It was a feat of engineering, yes. But it was also a feat of will.

So often we think a dream is the important thing. But whether Edison ever actually said that thing about inspiration versus perspiration, he certainly lived it. The lightbulb was not that much of a breakthrough—what Edison did through sheer will and determination was discover, after combing the ends of the earth, what kind of filament would make the invention commercially viable. Even this was irrelevant without the next part, figuring out just exactly how he would manage not only to generate sufficient electricity to power even a single city block of homes, but how he would deliver it to each one.

Belshaw had dreamed of the road but, more essentially, he had carved it out of the face of the earth. He had made a real dent in the universe. You could literally see it, the sharp breaks of dynamite blasting appeared every few meters. But to do so, he had to strike a devil's bargain with nature. She'd give him the tools and the path to build his road. But periodically, she'd collect her toll, wash it all away, and force him to begin again.

I stay in the same cabin where Belshaw once lived. Right in the middle of town. I've put my own touches on it, but Belshaw's portrait still hangs in one corner of the room. I wonder if he was ever stranded from getting back to his own cabin. Was he humble about his creation, aware of its ephemerality? Or was he like Xerxes, the great Persian king, who once sent a threatening letter to a mountain that looked like it would crumble and block his path and, on another occasion, in a fit of rage, ordered that lashes be delivered to a river that had destroyed a bridge needed by his army?

Famine is awful. The feast was somehow worse. I had been begging for water, hoping nature would turn on the spigot, but I never thought about what too much would do. I had no idea how to turn the hose off.

What has the power to create also has the power to destroy. They say that after a flood, no one drop of rain feels responsible. But that's how it can work with big projects. You can get to a point of death by a thousand paper cuts. And when I saw what was once our road illuminated by my headlights after a long day of running around, I was done. I had worked too hard, for too long, to have something like this happen.

I returned to my truck and put my hands on the side of my head, my elbows on my steering wheel and just sat there. It might have been an hour, it might have been a few. I thought about the months I had spent clearing the debris of the hotel under spotlights until two or three A.M. Or the dozens of runs it took to bring the blocks up the hill. The spills. The breakdowns. All the different people who had pushed so hard for this to happen. It seemed like all that work was for nothing. We were pushing to get this completed before the winter, and now there was no timeline on getting it done. I was crushed by the unfairness of it all.

These days, the legalities of the road to Cerro Gordo are a complicated matter, but because the Department of Water and Power has a communications tower above the town it's technically a utility road. And a utility road is maintained by the county.

This is good and bad. It's good because the maintenance of an eight-mile rural dirt road built in a wash is the responsibility of the county and so, the liability is on them. If someone sends their car off the cliff . . . not my road. The downsides are that I cannot put up a gate stopping people from coming up to town. And when it comes to maintaining the road, I have to get clearance from the county before touching it. It is a final irony of the story between Cerro Gordo and L.A.'s Department of Water and Power that we now have to coordinate with them for all help related to access to the town.

And given that Inyo County is the second largest county in California by land mass, and seems to own only one or two motor graders, it could be a while before anything gets fixed. The county has roads through Death Valley National Park up to Whitney Portal. A highway to get to the uber popular Mammoth Lakes ski resorts. The little old road to Cerro Gordo is simply not that high on the priority list.

The rain had stopped. I had managed to make it back to my cabin, Belshaw's cabin, by taking a very remote and challenging back road through Death Valley National Park. It is approximately forty miles to get home compared to the eight the Yellow Grade normally is. Soon enough I was trying to get back to the mountain of tasks before me, and that meant that I had to navigate my way down the devasted sluice that the road had become. As I gingerly drove down the mountain, I tried to make sense of it all. I had already tackled the first stage of grief—denial—on my way up the mountain during the storm, and I had breezed through the middle three steps. Now I had finally reached the stage of acceptance. As my dirt bike rattled and banged along, I started to take a mental inventory of everything we had at our disposal, as well as the steps that would be needed to get moving again. Rebuilding the road was not just inevitable, it was part of Cerro Gordo's history. And if I was going to be the next guy to write my name into the town's history, how could I not expect to have to rebuild the road?

Often in life, you have to accept reality, for better or worse. You can resent it or you can embrace it. And once you embrace it, you can see it as an opportunity to see what you're really made of.

I was, I realized, buried up to my waist in opportunity, all of which had been washed down the mountain by the storm.

I also realized that it's a lot easier to hoist a metric ton of opportunity when you have the right tools to lift it. Serendipitously, somebody had left exactly the tool I needed parked nearby—a SANY excavator. A big boy, the SY500H. The type of machine that can take out an entire hillside in fifteen minutes, including a ten-minute break for coffee. My friends Heavy D Sparks and Diesel Dave had left the excavator there, as we had just finished installing the forty-thousand-gallon water tank. I was fortunate to have a number of great volunteers at the town at the time, too. Scotty, Phil, and an old lizard of a man named Red.

When Dave left, he gave very clear instructions that nobody was to use the excavator except me. Those things retail close to $400,000, so leaving it behind was quite the act of trust. And in retrospect, a miracle in many ways.

"Dave, I need the excavator for a few more days."

"Of course, man. What's going on?"

"Road is gone; we got wiped out in this flood."

"Nooooo. Do we need to come back out? We're busy but I can rally the guys."

"I think we've got it. I could just use a couple more days before they pick up the machine."

"Done. Call me if you need backup."

Dave's generosity knows no bounds, and the fact that he was not only willing to allow us to use the excavator but potentially come back speaks to his character. The timing of it already being in town was another blessing.

If I was in the excavator, we'd need someone else in another piece of machinery. Red knew how to work almost anything like it was his second nature, so I figured I'd rent a backhoe and have Red start working where I couldn't. In between us, we'd have Scotty and Phil moving any exceptionally large rocks out of the way, as well as raking the dirt to make it a bit smoother if needed.

As I was pacing around the property, I was feeling pretty good about my plan. It was going to be a lot of work, but we'd proven time and time again we were up to that task, and this was no different. The sand had been messed up, and we were participating in the timeless tradition of rebuilding it once more.

The only thing that could put a stop to these plans was the county. I'd have to get their permission before doing anything further.

"Ten weeks. We got Highway 136 completely wiped out, dirt across half of 395, and a thousand people still missing in the park. I love Cerro Gordo, but we're just too slammed."

The road supervisor for Inyo County was doing his best, but the best was ten weeks before they anticipated being able to get our road open again. Ten weeks without any hotel progress. Ten weeks with no clear-cut way to even get home. Ten weeks would put us into winter. Winter would set us back another six months. Nearly a year of progress on the town hinged on getting this road opened up. Ten weeks wasn't going to work.

I knew where he was coming from. I could imagine the stress he was under. Paved roads in Death Valley National Park were crumpled up into gravel. Over one million people per year visit Death Valley. Almost three thousand every single day. The main roads in and out of the park were toast. More than one thousand people were missing somewhere inside the park. Highway 395, the main road into Lone Pine, Bishop, Mammoth Lakes, and Yosemite, was overrun with debris and mudslides. Tens of thousands of people per day were having their travel plans interrupted. An old town with a few residents couldn't take priority.

"What if I took the excavator and went down and worked on it a bit myself?"

A long pause.

"It's OK with me because we are spread thinner than thin can be right now."

That was a big deal. A sign of trust from the county that after years of working hard on the town, they knew I could be trusted to repair a difficult and dangerous country road. Out here there are no HOA fees. No coverage when things go wrong. You learn to rely on your fellow man in a way that never seems to happen in cities. Out here it can literally be life or death. And catastrophes, as bad as they are, can bring people together.

In 1872, an earthquake hit outside of Lone Pine, triggering a massive lake-bound tsunami in Owens Lake, which killed twenty-six people and leveled most of the buildings in Lone Pine. When news got up to Cerro Gordo, the residents there raised $800 (about $20,000 in today's money) to help their neighbors down in Lone Pine. When the county was slammed, they allowed me to get to work. To get the road passable again.

As I started up the excavator and crept down the Yellow Grade Road toward the narrows, I thought of the Buddhist monks and their mandalas. They spend hours, days, months, creating beautiful designs, just to wipe them clean and start over once they're finished. The sand is removed, brought back to nature, and the process begins again. They approach each new beginning with grace, do it well, do it beautifully.

Sometimes in big projects there are not finish lines but processes. You can get angry, you can let it drive you nuts. Or you can learn to love it. See it all as a mandala—a work of art.

FIRE

The main battle each day is getting warm and figuring out how to stay warm. It's a fight that begins on the back foot for me since I sleep in the smallest room inside the Belshaw House, which is fairly easy to keep warm with a small radiator heater and an electric blanket.

So I wake up warm, but as soon as I emerge from the room, the coldness of the rest of the untamed house confronts me with the truth of life at 8,500 feet, as if the warmth of a good night's sleep was a lie that I had personally perpetrated.

The first order of business is to "break the morning cold." You have to get the first fire of the day going as quickly as possible. This will raise the overall temperature of the house for long enough that by the time the fire has died down, the sun has reached the town and begun to do the rest of the work of heating everything up.

It's a good plan, but it only sometimes works. On days when the clouds roll in, when the snow falls, when the wind doesn't let up, attempts to heat the house are ongoing. Cold air races through the cracks in the wall as quickly as the wood tries to heat the space. It's a constant battle that can sometimes consume the entire day, and while it is never definitively lost, it is almost never won. Before the cold is "broken," the sun sets, night settles in, and I have to retreat to my room with the electric blanket and the heater as my armor and shield.

Those are the days I dream of installing central heat. There's something romantic about battling the elements.

There's something beautiful about observing a frigid winter's day outside.

But it's only romantic when you win the battle, and it's only beautiful outside when it's warm and cozy inside. When you don't, and it's not, then it's just brutal and no amount of fire in the stove or the fireplace is enough.

Every day, every fire is a bit different. It depends on the type of wood, the age of the wood, and the person lighting the fire. It's very tempting on the coldest mornings, when you can barely feel your hands, to overload the fireplace with wood, knowing that more wood means more fuel, which means more heat. But that is a certain way for the fire to never catch. The wood needs space, oxygen, to really get burning. It's a visual, visceral reminder each morning of the importance of making space, holding space. In life. In work. In love.

Sitting beside a carefully tended fire on a cold night in a place like Cerro Gordo, it's easy to forget your troubles. To be mesmerized by the dancing flames and allow your imagination to wander. To believe that you're in control. That you were the one that stacked the wood, you are the one who puts more in, so it's up to you to dictate how fast and hot a fire burns. It's intoxicating. A well-made fire gives off more than just warmth and light. It gives off comfort. A sense of connection to the moment, to the place, to a past that isn't really your own.

It is, after all, the most ancient of our rituals. The art of making fire. It's the thing that set us apart from all the other beasts, the thing that, more than anything else, made us human and gave us the excuse to believe we were the masters of this world.

Most of us have lost sight of that in our modern world. Fires still burn all around us, but most of the time they're hidden, concealed in the core of distant power plants, or contained within the cylinders of automobile engines, or tamed and neutered and flickering on our stove tops. Like so many things, we imagine that we've so thoroughly domesticated fire that we forget how powerful a fire can be. And then, from time to time, it reminds us. A siren shrieking down city streets in the night, an acrid cloud of choking smoke roiling against a red sky in a tinder-dry forest in the far northwest. Fire defies us, it escapes our control and teaches us that it is far more of a force of nature than we can imagine, far more than any single one of us can ever be.

That, too, is a lesson I learned the hard way in Cerro Gordo.

CHAPTER 9

WHEN IT'S ALL GONE

The heat woke me up. A scorching wave of it roiled into my house and through my room like the aftershock of a bomb blast. Hotter, at least in my mind, than anything I had experienced even on the worst day of summer in Death Valley.

My room had been turned into a furnace. And after one came another; wave after wave of superheated air pummeled me. Even my skin felt hot, and the waves felt like they were tugging at me like an undertow in an ocean, only these waves seemed to be coming straight from hell.

Then I heard crackling and popping, almost like gunshots. In the confusion that came with being awoken at three o'clock in the morning, I thought for a moment that maybe some of the troublemakers from down in the outskirts of Keeler had come to town firing off guns. It wouldn't have been the first time that happened. But rubbing my eyes and staring out my window, I realized that no, this was something far more dangerous than hopped-up desert dwellers with too much time and too many guns on their hands.

Jumping from my bed, I raced to the front room window that looks out on Cerro Gordo Road.

I didn't even need to pull back the yellowed lace curtains to see it. A hundred feet up the road, behind the bunkhouse, past the old theater that once upon a time had been a church, the entire hillside was aglow. It wasn't an easy steady glow; it was raging and out of control, pulsing furiously, red and orange. There was a fire in town.

I stepped out onto the porch and a flying ember of comprehension lighted on me. That popping I had heard. It was the sound of superheated cans exploding, of ancient timbers being decimated in the flames. A wave of hot terror hit me. Cerro Gordo is a ghost town, sure, but there were still gas lines and electrical lines in town. There are many old and dry and wooden buildings just standing there, one next to the other.

What if the flames reached them?

It took me a few precious seconds to orient myself. In my earlier confusion, I had thought that the fire was somewhere behind the bunkhouse, but I soon realized that it had just been a trick of the light, the way the glow had reflected off the walls of the canyon. The fire was in the opposite direction.

It was the American Hotel.

The centerpiece of Cerro Gordo, the cornerstone for everything I had planned to build in this place, was completely engulfed. I looked up and prayed this was all a nightmare.

It was. But it was real. I couldn't tell if it was the smoke or the magnitude of the tragedy, but tears streamed down my face.

The American Hotel was the first place I truly fell in love with when I came to town. Two stories, with wraparound porches that overlooked the entire valley. You could just feel the care that went into building it back in the day, the way each plank of its cedar clapboard siding had been hand-planed by someone who clearly cared about the place as much as I did. The years had robbed the clapboard of its luster, aging the planks so that when I arrived they had all taken on the patina of old cedar shakes, a touch of Old New England in the Southwestern desert. You could see the loving craftsmanship in the way the bar had been carved, and how so many hands over so many years had worn it smooth. You could feel it in the millwork in the tiny upstairs bedrooms, and you almost believed that the woodwork there had absorbed a thousand secrets over the years, secrets it would keep for as long as it stood. You could feel it in the milled posts that supported the roof over the second-floor balcony, and you could imagine some traveler resting his hand against one of those posts as he gazed out at the spectacular view of the Owens Valley and Mount Whitney before him.

I've always loved learning lesser-known history, hunting for obscure treasures, giving over my imagination to clues to lost stories. To me, the American Hotel was the embodiment of the romance of that kind of discovery. Victor Beaudry's general store was Cerro Gordo's time capsule, sure, but the American Hotel was time itself. It didn't contain history, like a museum; it was history, like a monument. Tens of thousands of fortune-seekers had passed through its front doors, eaten from its kitchen, slept in its rooms, gotten drunk in its saloon, and made bets, deals, promises at its tables. The American Hotel was the heart of Cerro Gordo. It was at the heart of our plans for the town's future.

Every stick of wood in the place was carefully chosen and handled and placed. Together, they made the place look venerable.

They also made it vulnerable.

I fumbled for my cellphone and punched in 911.

"Hello, 911, what's your emergency?"

"A fire. At Cerro Gordo Mines. We have a fire here."

"What's the address?"

"Cerro Gordo Mines. Above Keeler. It doesn't have a postal address."

"Ohhhh. Up there. OK, I'll get them up there as quick as I can."

My heart sank. Even under the best of circumstances, there was little chance that any help would arrive in Cerro Gordo before the fire completely incinerated the American. The closest fire station was in Keeler, a town with just forty souls and a volunteer fire department. There was another station, a long stretch of miles away in Lone Pine, but they, too, were volunteers. And farther away in Olancha, there was yet another fire station. God knows how many volunteers could be mustered or how long that would take, and even if every one of them showed up, they'd still have to make it up the rutted eight-mile road to Cerro Gordo with fire trucks and equipment that was never intended to traverse that kind of terrain. On the best day, I can coax my dirt bike up the hill in twenty minutes or so. Those trucks were going to take hours.

There's a deep pain that comes when you realize you will likely not be rescued. Your mind battles your heart, trying to convince it of ways it can work out. Your heart knows nothing will ever be the same.

Crying, delirious, and turned around, I went looking for the help we did have. Robert, the former caretaker, was in town, having returned the previous day for the first time since he had gone to care for his ailing wife. By the time I reached his cabin, the inferno had already spread and was beginning to consume the Ice House attached to the rear of the hotel. Next door, the Crapo House, named for the man who built it (and later murdered someone right outside its front door), was already gone. Robert's cabin was right beside those, a subtle wind shift away from erupting into flames itself.

Robert was behind the wheel of his truck, backing out of his driveway when I got there.

I thought he was fleeing.

"Where the hell are you going?!" I screamed at him. Robert couldn't hear me. His windows were rolled up, shielding him from the searing heat. He wasn't fleeing. He was responding. The fire had gotten so hot it melted the truck's tail lights and Robert was worried that flames might start licking at the gas tank, turning the truck into a giant Molotov cocktail.

Water was the only thing on my mind. The water pump from the mine had not yet been repaired and so I dashed through town, searching for every bucket I could find, any gallon jug undrank. It was only luck that we had any at all. A few weeks prior to the fire, I had decided Cerro Gordo needed more life, so we got a few goats. Those goats needed water and so we had stashed a hundred gallons or so next to their pen. Thank God for thirsty goats.

Robert and I threw ourselves against the fire. My friends Aaron and Nick, who happened to be in town that night, did, too. I don't know how long we battled futilely against the blaze. We didn't even bother to try to stop it in the places where it was already burning, instead we turned out attention to protecting the buildings that were in the path of the fire, like the Gordon House, dousing the fire as it snaked along the ground with buckets full of water until we ran out of that supply, stamping out embers where we saw them land. As a last-ditch effort, we grabbed gallon jugs of Crystal Geyser water, tore off the lids and squeezed the contents out on the smoldering ground fires. At best, the fire only hissed briefly when we'd douse it, and then continued on its way. The heat was so strong, so in control of the atmosphere, that sometimes the water never even made it to the ground, evaporating in midair before it ever touched the flames. And when we ran out of bottled water, we grabbed shovels and carved rudimentary firebreaks into the earth to prevent the blaze from advancing.

You know that it's making no difference. But the thought of just standing there is too horrible to consider.

It was nearly five A.M. before the first fire truck arrived in Cerro Gordo, almost two hours after my panicked 911 call. The fire had made it to within ten feet of the Gordon House, one of the most ornate in town, originally built by L. D. Gordon after he discovered zinc here and breathed new life into Cerro Gordo. The house was a time capsule, filled with relics and treasures. Some of its shingles were already singed. But it was saved.

Losing it could have meant losing the rest of the town, as the fire would have spread even farther up canyon.

The same could not be said for the American. The careful carpentry, the precise, loving placement of every piece of wood, had given the place a kind of magical charm, a warmth and a beauty. But it had also inadvertently been built to burn. Insulated with hundred-year-old newspaper, built to allow the air to flow just enough in just the right places, when flames touched the dry, aged wood, it set off a conflagration.

I sat, exhausted. And as the gray morning slithered in, the full scope of the disaster came into focus. Disaster. Even the word we use to describe devastation and loss is forged in fire. It literally means a disorder among the stars, as if these distant balls of fire in the sky somehow have agency over our fate.

My hopes, my dreams, and my life savings literally went up in flames in front of me. I was emotionally charred. Every negative emotion I'd ever felt in my life, I'd just felt ten times more strongly, concentrated into two hours. I felt disconnected from the world around me. Like in the moment before you go under for surgery, but stretched out over hours. Aaron, Nick, Robert, and I had fought the flames furiously, but for nothing, it seemed. The charred remains of the hotel, still smoldering, hissing and popping, lay in a grotesque pile. The air was full of the acrid stench of damp smoke and ash— that's what despair smells like.

The first thing your mind does when you see something so senseless, so tragic, is to look for something that makes sense. "Someone must have done this" feels easier to swallow than the possibility that lightning struck—either literally or figuratively. When something harms you, you want to believe that someone chose to do that, because somehow being the object of premeditated malice is more comforting than being the victim of random, terrible, merciless misfortune. I started to convince myself that this couldn't have been an accident. Not with this timing. Three A.M.? In the dead of the night? When nobody would be awake to see the proverbial match get struck? Less than two hours after my friend Nick had checked every building to make sure the lights were off and then had gone to bed? No way. My mind started racing and leaping between vague memories, trying to connect them like dots and hoping that the lines between them would reveal the face of a culprit. Had I made an enemy down the hill in Keeler that I didn't even know about? Did I look at someone the wrong way at the gas station outside Lone Pine and that perceived slight blew up into this?

Just because you're paranoid doesn't mean someone isn't also out to get you. I knew that the locals didn't trust me yet. I was still an outsider to them. An interloper. The newspaper articles about the sale of the town called us an investor group from L.A. who, they probably assumed, threw money at the previous owners so we could breeze in and out whenever we wanted in order to play Indiana Jones up in the mountains for a little while. Eventually, they all figured, I would get bored and go back to my real life like the rest of the city folks who came before me.

Maybe one of these locals was trying to drive me out.

It's even easier to consider yourself. Had I done something? Worse, had I not done something?

We'd rather be reckless, we'd rather fuck up, than to stare at sheer and random fate, at an indifferent world, where everything we care about can be blackened beyond recognition before our eyes.

A hot coal of guilt started to burn in my gut.

One of the reasons the previous owners sold Cerro Gordo to me, over other buyers with higher offers, was that I had promised to be a steward of the town, a minder of the mines, a guardian of the history. And yet, this happened. Even if my fevered paranoid fantasies had been right, even if it was an intruder who set the fire, it had still happened on my watch.

I tumbled back to my cabin and collapsed on the rocking chair.

The only thing that got me out of the chair was the steady stream of locals now making their way up the road from down in the valley.

News travels fast in small towns. Bad news travels like a bullet. There are no secrets in a place where everybody knows everybody, where everybody's father or brother or ex-girlfriend serves on the local volunteer fire company. And so they streamed into town, some with looks of real compassion etched in their faces, a few casting suspicious glances my way. The gathering took on the feeling of a wake. But I was not, in their minds, the bereaved. To many of them, I was still an interloper, and between their rote expressions of condolences, I could see that they were studying me, trying to determine whether this blaze would melt my resolve or whether it would steel me.

Would I, having lost the most precious part of my plans for the rejuvenation of Cerro Gordo, cut and run as they suspected, or would I stay and do everything in my power to make this place rise from the ashes?

At that point, I don't think I knew the answer to that myself.

The universe is a trickster, a cruel taskmaster with a wicked and grotesque sense of humor. And as I sat there, my body upright but my heart in the fetal position, my cellphone started to buzz with text messages, not of condolence but of congratulations.

"Just saw the piece. It's great. Congrats, dude!"

"Mmm what a sweet story. CG looks unbelievable. I gotta get up there!"

What the hell are they talking about?

Then I realized, that very day, that worst day of my life, the *New York Times* had decided to run a story about my time at Cerro Gordo. Beginning months earlier, I had talked a number of times with a young freelance writer who had a passion for old ghost towns in the West. She told me she planned to pitch it to the *Times* as a follow-up to a story they had done earlier when we bought Cerro Gordo. I never thought much about it. I'd been around enough journalists to know pieces often fall apart. I figured it would never see the light of day. Still, talking with the writer—Angella—helped me focus my thoughts, sharpen my plans, and stoke my own passion for the place.

But now, here it was. In all its glory at the moment of my deepest despair, a front-page story in the Style section, complete with a front-page picture of me, decked out like a crazy cowboy, rawhide jacket, full beard, and all, sitting right there in the middle of the picture with a bottle in my hand at the table in the old poker room. Behind me there was a hole in the wall, rumored to be from a bullet. Below that, a suspicious mass of stain, rumored to be blood. I was happy. I was hopeful. I was frozen in time.

Everything in that picture was gone now. Everything, that is, except me.

Had fate decided to prod the editors at the *Times* to publish that story that very day to taunt me, or to drive me to action? I had no idea.

A profound sadness set in. The deeply personal kind that you can't share with anyone no matter how much you talk about it with them. Because even if you went through the same traumatic experience, this kind of sadness isn't related to the physical loss you share; it comes from the loss of its meaning in your life, which only you can know. This kind of sadness bubbles up to fill the void left by meaning, and if you're not careful, it does so very quickly and very completely.

Before you know it, you're drowning in a pit you didn't even realize had been dug. One dug right from your heart.

I retreated inside. I went into my room, shut the door, turned off my phone, lay down on the bed, and closed my eyes. I was exhausted.

Physically and emotionally. I needed to rest, but sleep wasn't happening. Behind my eyelids I didn't find the familiar starry darkness that greets you right before sleep; I saw only fire. I saw the American Hotel burning. I saw myself asleep. I saw bright orange, blood red, and the eerie blue-gray hue of smoke billowing up through darkness. I saw myself frantic and helpless. I saw the fire, fiendish and ceaseless.

And just as my own white-hot grief was about to consume me, hope knocked.

More specifically it was Sean Patterson, the previous owner of the town, knocking on my door. He lived in Bakersfield now, but when he heard the news, he jumped in his truck and headed two hundred miles north. As soon as I saw him, my grief was compounded with shame.

I was sure he'd be furious, disgusted—with me and with himself for trusting me. I'd failed him. I'd failed every owner preceding him, including the namesake of the home in which I was currently standing.

Instead, he hugged me.

I burst into tears. I sobbed. Great, heaving paroxysms of grief and loss; the kind that little kids have when they're tired and frustrated and can't find their words. Sean put his arm around me and sat me down in one of the chairs on the porch.

"I'm so sorry," I croaked, my voice raspy from smoke and the bitter ash of my own failure.

"It's too early to know for certain, but based on the way things burned it looked electrical."

I stared at the floor. So? What does it matter? I had lost the hotel. It was my failure. But he grabbed me, a little roughly, the way a father might when he sees his son slipping into despair, and he looked into my eyes until he was sure I understood what he was telling me.

"This wasn't your fault, Brent," he continued. "It was bound to happen."

I did not understand it then. In time I would. Fire has always been a part of the story of Cerro Gordo. Like floods and droughts, fire has, in its way, shaped the place. Indeed, in some ways, fire made Cerro Gordo. It began at the beginning of time when that fiery furnace deep in the earth sent fingers of molten silver and zinc rising toward the surface. This whole town exists because of the riches forged in that primordial inferno and left in its wake. And since then, time and again, fire has left its mark on this place. Of the four hundred buildings that once stood here in Cerro Gordo's heyday, only about twenty remain. Those that do are, I suppose, the beneficiaries of a kind of Darwinism: They've survived literal trial by fire.

There was the fire in 1877 that burned the brand-new hoisting works over the Union Mine shaft and nearly killed thirteen miners working seven hundred feet and nine hundred feet underground.

Like the American Hotel, the hoist house went up in flames incredibly fast. Within minutes of the town's fire alarm sounding, the local newspaper reported, "the whole of the large structures . . . were in flames." The fire ended up burning four hundred cords of fuel wood, five or six nearby cabins, and all the machinery in the hoist house itself except for the boiler, which one can assume survived only because fire was, by design, its natural element.

It was only the quick thinking and downright heroism of the mine's superintendent, a man named Porter, and the courageous actions of the men in his charge, that saved the miners working below and potentially countless others. Porter sent a group of men 190 feet down into the mine directly underneath the fire and had them build a horizontal barrier of timber and rock across the main mineshaft to prevent the fire from getting sucked down to the auxiliary shafts. Had it reached that point, the miners trapped below would have no way of escaping. At the same time, a little farther down the main shaft, another group of men deliberately caved in one of the stopes where they were storing the dynamite used to blast their way deeper into the mountain.

Had those crates ignited, there is no telling what the damage to the mine would have been or what the loss of life would have looked like.

In fact, even beyond the confines of Cerro Gordo, fire is more than just a fact of life, it's a driver of life, a prime mover of sorts. This whole part of the country is, in a way, an heir to fire. There are species of pine trees that grow in the American West that owe their survival entirely to fire. Only in the extreme heat of a raging blaze can the pinecone for those trees open, allowing their seeds to find a footing in the earth and creating out of destruction a new cycle of life. The phoenix rising from the ashes isn't just a myth, it's a critical fact to which entire species of trees owe their existence.

All of these conflicting thoughts were caroming into one another in my brain—the grief, the loss, the consolation that comes from the first flickering recognition that all of it is part of a cycle of destruction and rebirth—when Sean spoke again, and roused me from my daze.

"This fire is part of Cerro Gordo's story now," he said. He was right. Soon it wouldn't be news anymore. It wouldn't be a business problem. Sooner than I was probably ready for, it wouldn't belong to me or my story either. It would be history. The Fire of 2020. An event, a tragedy, an accident in a long series of events that made Cerro Gordo into more than a town, part of the legend and the mystery of a place that had been forged by fire.

"You can't change what happened," Sean said finally. "But what happens next is up to you."

Meaning, the fire, the loss, the story in the *Times* that morning, all of it could overwhelm me, or I could find fire-born riches in myself and do what nature and Cerro Gordo demanded.

I suppose I already knew it before Sean ambled off my porch that morning. Fire had ravaged Cerro Gordo and robbed me of the most precious jewel the town had offered me. But what happened next was entirely my choice. I would reclaim what the fire had taken, I would make good on the promises I had made. I would rebuild the American Hotel. I'd recover its lost magic and glory, but I'd build it back better. The New American Hotel would be stronger than the old, and it would be so because its future had been born of fire.

Sean hadn't just pardoned me for a sin, he had inspired me, and for that I will always be in his debt. The power of his compassion, of his clemency, of his grace—it was as invaluable to me as it is immeasurable.

As it happened, there are always small mercies in even the worst moments. Just a few days before, Nick and I had discovered the blueprints for the hotel and, for no discernible reason, we decided to move them out of the building. We had no way of knowing then that we had effectively saved the seed corn for the new hotel.

While walking toward the back room of the Belshaw House to find the plans, I thought about another old piece of paper I had recently been emailed—a newspaper article announcing the birth of the American Hotel.

It was dated June 15, 1871, precisely 149 years to the day that the American Hotel burned to the ground. The day that the old American Hotel perished in flames was the very same day that it had come into the world, in a dazzling celebration complete with a glorious fireworks display. In grief and in glory, fire always plays a part.

Now I had a part to play.

There was no one around but myself and the ghosts of Cerro Gordo. To them, to no one, I said aloud, "I will rebuild this hotel before its one hundred and fiftieth birthday."

How hard could that be?

CHAPTER 10

BE YOUR OWN LIGHT

The fire of 1877. The fire of 1880. The fire of 1912. There had been so many fires that they didn't name them all. The fires had begun for many reasons, they each had burned in their own unique, horrible ways—claiming lives, destroying buildings, taking history with them even as they met it.

The aftermath was similar each time—the owners, the workers, the investors decided what to do next.

"What happens next is up to you," Sean had said.

So it had gone at Cerro Gordo for a century and a half; so it goes in the aftermath of every disaster and setback.

What are you going to do about it? What comes next?

The Fire of 2020 was now its own part of history, as much as all the catastrophes of the past, and it was my task, my obligation, to dutifully and accurately preserve every terrible detail for posterity. I had taken it upon myself to be the guardian and curator of the history of Cerro Gordo, and that meant that now, in the absolute depths of my despair, I was honor-bound to record the devastation, and to detail, with all the brutal honesty I could summon, my own sense of loss and grief.

It is not easy to share the worst moment of your life, even with those closest to you. It's harder still to share it with people who are, so you imagine, strangers.

How could I make anyone else understand the torment I was going through at that moment?

The acrid stench of my own worst nightmare still lingering in the wake of the fire? How could I express the guilt I felt, despite Sean's compassionate pardon? How could I share my own self-doubt about whether I had it in me to rise to the challenge and rebuild the American Hotel, and with it my dreams for Cerro Gordo's future?

In my earlier public, social media pronouncements about Cerro Gordo, I had managed to get a small group of strangers in various far-flung places around the globe to believe that they, too, had a kind of stake in what happened here. Would they feel that I had betrayed them, let them down, failed them when the American burned to the ground?

The American Hotel was my pride and my joy. And it was theirs, too. Every vision I had for Cerro Gordo revolved around it. They had shared those visions. And now it was destroyed.

"What happens from here is up to you," Sean had said.

I plumbed the depths of myself, hoping to find the strength to break the news of the catastrophe.

I came up short. It took every ounce of strength I had to force myself to walk the short distance to the general store, set up a tripod, and push record on my Sony a7 camera. I had borrowed that camera because somewhere along the line I thought I might want to take up astrophotography, to take family portraits of the stars. Now I was using it to document a disaster.

"The fault . . . is not in our stars, but in ourselves," says Cassius in Shakespeare's *Julius Caesar.* He and Sean ought to get together for a coffee or a beer someday. They have a lot in common.

I panned the scorched landscape with the camera, then turned the camera toward myself to try to explain.

Before I could even spit out the first word, I choked up.

"About . . ." I kept trying to speak but the words just weren't coming.

"About five hours ago . . ." And then sobbed.

I forced myself to speak. Simple. Clear. Direct. Every word was its own ordeal. But I had to push through.

"About five hours ago around two or two-thirty in the morning, a fire burned down our hotel here at Cerro Gordo," I said. Then the words started to come, slowly at first, but then more steadily, the way a small, warming fire on a cold morning stops sputtering and begins to grow strong.

"Last night I woke up to an explosion of the propane tank in the hotel," I said.

"I called 911 around three A.M. and by that point the hotel was essentially gone."

The words were coming steady now. There was something comforting in being able to speak about the unspeakable tragedy that had unfolded. I gathered my camera and strode down to the gutted remains of the hotel. This film would be a document of the disaster, but it would also, one day, when the American Hotel was rebuilt, be a reminder of how far we had come. I focused on an old wood stove from the hotel dining room that lay melted and mangled in the smoldering wreckage.

"This was the beautiful wood-burning stove in the middle of the hotel," I intoned from behind the camera.

I continued, every step a stumble across a charred piece of the hotel's storied past. I could still feel the residual heat from the blaze through the soles of my shoes. I needed to document everything.

"This would've been towards the kitchen, the beautiful cast-iron stove," I said.

"There's the refrigerator," I narrated as I pointed the camera at a mishappen hulk of metal and plastic that no longer bore any resemblance to a kitchen appliance.

I walked a bit farther and scanned the wreckage. It was all too much. I was once again feeling overwhelmed and defeated by the magnitude of the destruction.

I turned off the camera to walk back up toward the Belshaw. I needed to lie down.

"What happens from here is up to you."

Halfway home, Sean's words once again stopped me. I set up the tripod and the camera, and spoke directly to it.

"I'm not giving up. I'm going to die at Cerro Gordo," I bluntly declared. I suppose that sounds melodramatic. It wasn't meant to be. It was just a statement of fact, that my life and the life of this place were now, permanently, forged together. Fire does that.

If I was going to document every detail of the Great Cerro Gordo Fire of 2020, I had to document everything, including what was going on in my own heart.

"This isn't a start-up; I don't think of it in terms of month over month growth. The timeline here is decades. It's not years, it's not months. It's not days or hours."

This is bigger than me, I told the camera. If I were prone to flights of fancy, I might say that I don't believe it was even me talking to the camera that morning. I believe it was Cerro Gordo itself, speaking through me. I'm not that romantic. And, though, this deep into this book, this might surprise you, I'm not the type of guy who easily talks about his feelings, nor am I the kind of guy who normally reaches out to strangers. I'm a bit of an introvert, the kid in middle school who preferred to eat lunch alone. What kind of guy decides in the middle of his life to chuck it all and move to a ghost town in the middle of nowhere anyway? He's certainly not your usual back-slapper.

But with the title, the responsibility to speak for Cerro Gordo was transferred to me, and it was my obligation to speak now. To define in that moment Cerro Gordo's future.

"Cerro Gordo is going to be here after I'm gone, and there is going to be a hotel here."

That was it.

I was going to rebuild the hotel. It would stand again. I'd work until my hands bled if I had to. I was going on record, publicly, loudly proclaiming the whole process. Mapping out and documenting every step for the next few years. What happens next is up to me. And I was declaring that I was in the fight and would be to the bitter end.

I exposed myself in this video. I cried. I had, I imagined, looked weak, perhaps even a bit deranged. But I had committed myself, or, rather, recommitted myself to a task more daunting than anything I had ever faced before. This video was my contract with the future. And with the past.

I've found that if you connect with something larger than yourself, it helps overcome fears of sharing publicly. What I was pledging to do was for all the people who would ever come to Cerro Gordo in the years to come and it was for the thousands of people who lived in this town before I ever arrived here.

The firefighters were still tamping down the smoldering remnants of the old hotel when I finished my videotaped manifesto of hope. There was a stranger there, too—a sketchy, shifty little guy.

I watched from a distance as he pried up a small piece of wood, one cool enough to handle, and stuck it in his pocket. A souvenir of the Fire of 2020. I was pissed. In a moment like this? I calmed myself. The man was showing what Sean had said in words—this is part of Cerro Gordo's history. The man wanted a piece. I let him go.

When watching the flames the night before, I thought of Thomas Edison. In 1914, by chance or by negligence—you could never be sure which was which with Edison—his New Jersey factory erupted into flames. The blaze threatened to ignite hundreds of bottles of volatile chemicals that Edison kept on hand and when the inventor arrived on the scene, he found his son watching the blaze, paralyzed by confusion and terror.

Rather than turn his attention to the looming danger posed by the chemicals, which were now exploding and turning the flames into a fiendish rainbow, Edison grabbed his son by the shoulders and said, "Go get your mother and all her friends. They'll never see a fire like this again."

Humans have a fascination with tragedies. The gruesome. The

disasters. Who hasn't rubbernecked at a car accident along the highway? There is literally a global cottage industry focused on disaster tourism to satiate our macabre fascination with destruction on a massive scale. Even now, all these years after the disasters associated with them, people flock to the ruins of Pompei or the hills beneath Mt. St. Helens or the region around Chernobyl or to the Ninth Ward in New Orleans savaged by Hurricane Katrina. It's why they had to move the bus where McCandless died away from the Alaskan wilderness, because people have an insatiable desire to visit such places to see if they can still feel the aftershocks of disaster or tragedy.

Whether they know it or not, what those rubbernecks are really looking for is a shared experience that can only come in the wake of a terrible loss.

To put ourselves in each other's shoes. The shifty guy was able to dip his toe into the disaster site, to imagine dealing with an impossible situation. Thinking what he would have done differently. To take the emotions of such an event for a joy ride, without having to deal with any of the aftermath.

Understanding, empathy. It's what he was looking for and it's what I was looking for as I poured my heart out to my Sony a7. At the very least, I was capturing one of the worst and most broken moments of my own life so that I could look at it later. Hopefully from a better mental state.

I wandered back down to the hotel site.

I brought a magnet and began to drag it over the ashes. Black dust kicked up, I breathed it in and I could feel it sticking in the fibers of my lungs. This tragedy was now in me. A part of me.

Clink. Clink. Clink.

Nails started to come up.

Square nails, hand-forged. Each one slightly different. Their imperfections make each unique. Now charred, weakened, bent. Some I could break with just one hand. Others still looked like the day they were driven in. The wood that they had once held together was gone but here they remained.

I tossed them one by one into a steel tub.

With these nails, I would rebuild what I had lost. With these nails, I'd fasten together beams in the future hotel. I scanned the site. It was going to be a whole lot of work.

I was going to need help. I walked back up to my camera, grabbed it, and brought it down to the hotel site.

I pressed record again. Voice quivering, I barely got the words out.

One man had not built the hotel. Countless hands had built it and thousands more over the years had touched every corner of it, smoothing and shaping it into the place it had become.

One man alone could not rebuild it.

It would take a community.

"We're going to need a lot of help," I said. "We need people to help clean. We need people to help try to rebuild it."

"If you're close and have any type of construction skills or cleaning skills or even a truck to help move some stuff, we need the help, too. We need the manpower."

The full scope of the damage from the blaze was clearly visible behind me in the frame. A few hundred feet from where I stood there was still smoke billowing out of the charred remains of the hotel. Next to it lay a mangled knot of melted washing machines and the charred hunchback cadavers of what had been refrigerators, and beside that, the blackened crumpled sheets of corrugated steel that had been the roof. All these things that had to be cleared before any new construction could begin.

"I have this form we created to put in your info . . . I'd love to see some of you up here, helping out. I wish it was under better circumstances. But it's not."

Within hours of the blaze, my friend Aaron, who had originally sent me the listing to buy Cerro Gordo and who, by chance, was at the town the night of the fire, had set up a Google form where people could input their ability to help.

"This is a time when I know there are a lot bigger issues going on in the world and it seems silly to be asking for help with an old building. But it's an old building that means a lot to a lot of people." I was getting toward the end of the video and felt embarrassed, fully aware that we were in the middle of a pandemic where thousands of people were dying, and I was looking into the camera asking for help to rebuild part of a town that I owned.

"We're going to rebuild. What other option do we have? So I guess we've got to get to it." I stood up, revealing the entirety of the destruction behind me, walked forward, and turned off the camera.

I had it all down on tape; the devastation, the despair, the discovery of hope and the desperate plea for help. But I still wasn't sure that I had it in me to share it publicly. I sat up half the night debating with myself—with that kid who preferred to eat alone at the lunchroom table in middle school.

In the morning, I uploaded the video.

A few hours passed before I saw the first response. An old friend texted me.

"Saw the video. Pretty raw stuff. It's real. Authentic pain," he wrote.

The truth is, in the hours since I had posted the video, I hadn't had the heart to check my computer. Ordinarily, when I posted a video from Cerro Gordo it got a few hundred, maybe a few thousand views. I had built a community by that point, but it was a small one. I had no idea whether my video would move them at all, and if I'm being perfectly honest, when I saw my friend's text, I began to doubt that I had done the right thing. Had I shared too much? Had I been too emotional? Had I demanded too much of strangers? Somewhere deep inside I felt a twinge of shame for having been so open.

I stalked up to the wreckage of the hotel and threw myself into the work of cleanup, hoping to drown out the sound of my own doubts with the din of hard labor.

But even the work couldn't keep me away from returning to my room and turning on the computer. I had to see what I believed would be a handful of hateful comments cementing my shame.

The first comment flickered across the screen.

"I'm so sorry for your loss. I know that you'll rebuild."

"I'm taking off work tomorrow, what other supplies do you need?"

"Keep your head up!"

2,874 views. In a matter of a few hours, the video I had posted had gathered almost three thousand views. A group of strangers larger than any group I had ever been part of in the analog world had seen me at my weakest, literally sobbing on camera, a larger group than I have ever spoken to about anything at one time, had not only heard my pain but were sharing it, and for the most part they were rallying to my side.

There were the occasional trolls, vicious naysayers who took delight in my catastrophe, and wanted me to know that they blamed me for the catastrophe. Poor bastards. They didn't realize that nothing they could say about me was worse than what I thought about my own culpability for the fire.

"How could you all not have replaced ALL the wiring in the whole town when you bought the place?!" A good question and one that would haunt me for years to come.

Negative bias is a very familiar experience for anyone who's ever lived even a part of their life on social media. Even without the internet we tend to dwell on the negative longer than the positive. Supposedly this was an evolutionary adaptation to focus on threats, exaggerate the danger, and survive when we had lions trying to eat us. And since the negative takes more of our attention, we believe it to be true more often.

But for the most part, as I poured through the comments, I found words of encouragement, people offering materials and suggesting ideas to build back better and stronger. My plea had touched something in that community, and it was only a few hours before my lonely ordeal was blossoming into a collective mission.

Disasters can do two things—they can bond together or tear apart. And from early on, it seemed that this was bonding lovers of history together toward a common goal.

"DUDE, SO MANY people have signed up to volunteer, we have eight coming up tomorrow."

Aaron rushed into the Belshaw House to tell me that the volunteer form was swarming with support.

Fifty names.

Seventy-five names.

One hundred and fifty names.

More than a hundred people per hour were filling up our Google form to help out.

We sat up that night feeling energized, emailing back as many people as we could.

The very next day, eight people made their way up the Yellow Grade Road, eager to help in any way that they could. Five different people brought pickup trucks to help move debris.

Travis, from Orange County, even brought a dump trailer. The owner of the local tow company lent us a Bobcat tractor. A woman who drove four hours from Fresno came just to cook enchiladas for everyone. What looked to be an impossible hole to climb out of suddenly felt not only possible but achievable.

Afterward, I'd release many more videos. They included the progress of rebuilding the hotel, exploring abandoned mines, hosting group metal-detecting events, refining silver, and a lot more. In total, the videos would be seen over two hundred million times. Each week, I'd pour out my deepest fears about the project, my greatest accomplishments. I used the videos as a personal diary of the highs and lows of living in an abandoned mining town.

Each week, I shared a bit more and more of my hopes and dreams. I documented, sometimes obsessively, the progress of not just the hotel and other projects, but my personal growth as well. How much its progress (or lack thereof) affected me on a deeply emotional level. Millions of people saw me working late into the night, trying my best to see a town come back to life.

The more time I spent at Cerro Gordo, the more I fell in love with the town. And as my passion for Cerro Gordo burned brighter and brighter, more people warmed to our collective goal. What started as eight volunteers that first day grew to a dozen or so every weekend. Those volunteers in turn created their own history with the town and attracted more people. The idea of a group of people, no matter their background, rallying together, not just to save a piece of history but to write an entirely new history going forward was, well, there's no other word for it. It was inspiring.

Cerro Gordo was made by fire. Fire gave birth to it, fire wounded it again and again throughout its history and, in the Great Cerro Gordo Fire of 2020, it cleansed the land and, like those fire-dependent pine trees, it created the conditions under which an even greater Cerro Gordo could take root.

What this did in Cerro Gordo it also did in me. It cleared a path in me that allowed for future growth; it forced me to open parts of myself so that they could take root and grow.

The fire that ripped through Cerro Gordo and destroyed the American Hotel was the worst day of my life.

And for that, I will be eternally grateful to it.

Because it gave me a chance to be better. And it gave me a chance to build here, in this seemingly forsaken ghost town, a true community, bound not by geography, but by commonality.

That's the most precious thing ever mined in these mountains, and unlike all the other riches fashioned by fire and melted into ingots here, there is no end to that resource. It will never be played out until I am, until my virtual community is.

In the days since the blaze, hundreds of volunteers have made and continue to make the arduous trek to Cerro Gordo. Together we've worked on everything from repairing the old roofs to make sure rain didn't get it, hauling up materials for the new American Hotel, building new outhouses to handle the new traffic, even just organizing the toolshed. Every load carried, every hammer swung, is somebody staking a claim in Cerro Gordo. I've watched with absolute joy as each and every one of them fell in love with the town in the same way I did when I first moved up. It's one thing to see it online—in person they feel the magic of the town, learn a bit more about the history of the town, participate in the future of the town, and are surrounded by people doing the same. We tried to end each night with a group dinner, often around a campfire. There, too, fire creates something. Ever since the beginning of time, iron bonds of friendship have been formed in the flickering light of a fire ring.

And in that ancient art of building a fire, in that ancestral knowledge of how to precisely place the wood so the air can flow and the flames can be shared, there is the model for building everything—a hotel, a community, someday, perhaps, a starship that will travel light years between the fireballs in the night sky.

That video I made kindled a fire.

I was sharing my sense of pain, but also my sense of wonder. And that sense of wonder now burns in every heart in this far-flung community that has grown up around our shared endeavor.

I remember a couple weeks after the fire, I was down in Lone Pine having lunch with the county commissioner. We were eating at a table outside on the sidewalk, and I was updating him on our progress with the cleanup, when a young couple walking by recognized me and stopped to ask for a photo. This was very new to me, so I was just as confused as the commissioner about what was happening.

"What brings you to Lone Pine?" the commissioner asked them.

"We're big fans of the channel, and we thought we'd come visit and try to help."

"The channel?"

"I started a YouTube channel about the town," I told him sheepishly.

"Yeah, it's awesome!" one of them said.

"We weren't sure we'd get to meet you, Brent. This is the best."

"I'll see you up the hill then."

"See you there!"

I thanked them. The girlfriend gave me a hug. As they walked away, the significance of what just happened started to register with the county commissioner. Something was happening here.

Something good out of all this bad.

"Thank you for bringing your business to Owens Valley!" he shouted after them.

As more folks down the hill witnessed or heard about moments like that, the interests of the Cerro Gordo online community that I was building began to merge with those of the local community that I had inherited. Everyone was ready to help.

We each have it in us to bring a little fire into the world and to share that light with others.

When the Buddha was on his deathbed, his followers huddled around him and asked, "What are we going to do, now that you're leaving us?" To which the Buddha responded, "Be your own light!"

I never really understood that story until the afternoon after that raging conflagration at Cerro Gordo. It took an inferno to teach me how to keep my own fire burning and to show me how to joyfully share my own light and bask gratefully in the light of others.

CHAPTER 11

FIND YOUR SPARK

You have to give him credit for sheer orneriness. That kind of baked-in-the-sun madness that could make a man look five thousand feet up a rutted goat path that passed for a road, fix his gaze on the mountain, at a lawless, ramshackle mining camp sprawling out up there, a place with a murder a week, more rats than people, enough official corruption to make William Mulholland blush with shame, and no running water, and say to himself, "You know what? That place could certainly use a nice hotel. I think I'll build one there."

I guess men were made differently in 1870. Because back then, Mr. John Simpson set out to do just that. It didn't matter to him that every natural scrap of timber anywhere near Cerro Gordo had long since been cut and either used to shore up the mine shaft or burnt to keep the smelters running. Didn't matter to him that nails were as rare as hen's teeth, and every single one he'd need would have to be forged by hand.

This place was so remote that you'd have to travel days through the desert to one of those more civilized places like San Francisco to even find a blueprint for a decent hotel.

None of that mattered to him. None of that shook him off his dream. Not any more than those things had deterred the men who burrowed nine hundred feet through solid rock to build the mines at Cerro Gordo, not any more than it had stopped the men who built the fourteen-mile-long Salt Tram that allowed those intrepid old-timers to traverse some of the steepest terrain in the West, not any more than they had deterred Belshaw when he willed the Yellow Grade Road to the top of an impassable wash.

Simpson was just the latest of what by then was a long line of ornery, rattlesnake-tough visionaries who would let nothing stand between them and their dreams.

From the comparative comforts of the early twenty-first century, these men seem to be as hard as the land they lived on. Everything they did seems impossible to us now. Where did they find the money to build the things they built? Where did they find the resources in a place that had none to speak of, except for silver and the like? Where and how did they learn the skills they needed to wrestle this place into being, and, most important, where did they find in themselves the single-minded sense of purpose to make themselves do it? Just reading about their exploits is exhausting.

And yet, I suspect, a lot of you have the same stuff in you.

I once heard a speaker describe the ideal entrepreneur, the ideal founder, as a "high-agency person." "High-agency" is one of those Wharton-sounding words. The kind of thing I heard guys in the

Wall Street bars let out as they swirled their fourth martini. But there is something to it.

Even the least Wall Street guy Ralph Waldo Emerson said, "Shallow people believe in luck, believe in circumstances. . . . Strong men believe in cause and effect." In other words, high-agency people are the ones constitutionally unable to accept that the odds are stacked against them. They are the kind of people categorically unable to process the simple phrase "there's nothing you can do." The sort of people who absolutely and in perfect faith believe in their own power to change things or change their station in life.

In other words, people like John Simpson.

The history of Cerro Gordo is one of plunder and violence and audacity, sure. It's also filled with high-agency people, people who not only believed but proved that mountains could literally be moved by sheer will and competence.

Cause met effect. Agency was asserted.

Things got done.

Simpson is haunting me as I wander here, at the very top of Cerro Gordo, picking my way through the blackened-hull cadaver of his hotel. No, haunting is not the right word. He's taunting me, challenging me, trying to provoke me to action. Damn the odds, he's saying. You can do this, and you can do it easier than I could. You have better materials, more resources. You have at your fingertips the kind of stuff that I couldn't even dream of. If I had what you have, I would have been able to build a palace here, a cathedral, Notre Dame in the desert, with hot baths and towels for a nickel a throw. You can certainly rebuild my little hotel.

Maybe I need to make this clear. I did not actually hear John Simpson's voice. I may spend a good deal of my time alone in a ghost town, but I haven't spent enough time alone to start hearing the voices of men long dead. I may be getting colorful, but I'm not crazy. Not yet anyway.

But I can hear Simpson's voice loud and clear between the lines of that old yellowing newspaper clipping from the *Inyo Independent* that I had been sent not long after I got here.

"Mr. and Mrs. John Simpson, having established themselves in their new hotel, are prepared to accommodate the public, and respectfully solicit its patronage. Cerro Gordo, June 15, 1871."

How did they do it?

John Simpson didn't have big excavators, backhoes, and five-ton trucks to get things up the mountain.

But I do.

I did, however, have one obstacle that he didn't: modern building codes. When Simpson built his hotel, all he had to do was scratch out a path of ground and lay out his foundation on solid dirt. Modern sensibilities and the whims of bureaucracy made my task a little more complicated.

After spending weeks carting the remains of the old hotel offsite, I was obliged to submit signed, stamped, and sealed architectural and engineering plans. And those called for a proper, modern foundation. One that meant pouring eighty cubic yards of concrete.

The local contractors let me know that given the limitations of the road and the site, eighty cubic feet of concrete was an impossibility. The ghosts of John Simpson and his wife snickered over my shoulder. Nothing is impossible, they reminded me.

If I couldn't find a contractor to haul and pour my concrete, I'd find another way.

The issue, once again, was the Yellow Grade Road. Belshaw's middle finger to the idea that a man had limits. A man might not have limits. But Belshaw's road sure did. A fully loaded concrete truck weighs about 65,000 pounds. Filled, the truck will hold ten cubic yards of concrete. So—in an ideal world where we could drive fully loaded trucks up a steep grade—we were talking 520,000 pounds of trucks and concrete coming up our steep, off-camber, dirt road situated on the side of cliffs. Therein lies the rub. When a concrete truck goes up too steep of a grade, the concrete will fall out the back. If a truck gets too off-camber, it will tip over. At the weight these trucks would be coming in at, there were concerns that the 150-year-old cribbing (stacked rocks) supporting the road at the steepest cliffs would give way. I'm not diminishing the concerns of all those guys who turned me down when I asked them to haul my concrete. I might have said that, too, if it were my trucks that I was putting at risk.

But there's more than one way to skin a mule. We do, after all, live in a thoroughly modern world—we've not only figured out ways to navigate across the land, we've mastered the skies, as well. I remembered seeing videos of helicopters airlifting massive buckets of concrete and dumping them at the top of some mountain somewhere to lay the footings for a chairlift at a ski resort. Maybe I could do that here, I thought. The whole notion excited me, the thought of some chopper jockey hovering over the mountain like Robert Duvall in *Apocalypse Now,* blasting "Ride of the Valkyries" from a loudspeaker as he dumped a few tons of wet concrete from on high.

I'd never been in a helicopter. This could be cool, I thought.

And then I saw the price tag: $165,747. Plus a $6,000 per diem for the crew. And that didn't even include the entrance music. Nationwide, it costs about $125 a cubic yard for concrete delivered to the site. This was more than sixteen times that cost.

Scratch the chopper.

And so there I was. No trucks. No helicopters. Well, then, I'd do it the old-fashioned way. I'd tote it up there and mix it myself on-site. It only took forty ninety-pound bags of Quikrete to make a yard. So, what, 3,200 bags? I'd break open the bags one by one, mix it in a wheelbarrow, and call it a day. It would be a long and dirty job, but after more than a year of banging my head against the wall trying to convince contractors to come up, it seemed quicker than what I'd been doing.

But even that basic rudimentary approach had its problems. Turns out the higher-ups in California, even the ones who pretend that they're the direct inheritors of the old Wild West spirit, are still sticklers for doing things the modern way. That meant that the entire foundation had to be poured at once, as a single, structurally cohesive unit. A "monolithic pour." Building code and the bean counters demanded it.

Privately, I held out hope that somehow, someway, this concrete would get delivered—doing it myself was fantastically insane—but with each passing day, that seemed less and less likely. Then something began to happen. As I chased down dozens of fruitless leads, viewers of the channel started chiming in with ideas. When you have a healthy community of people watching a town come back to life, a certain percentage of those people are going to know a lot more than you do about whatever you're trying to do—concrete included. Some of them might even know someone who knows someone who could help you.

Almost daily I got comments and emails telling me what I should do. The vast majority of these suggestions did not understand some piece of the logistical puzzle; a small minority did have creative solutions, but the cost to execute would have been more than the helicopter company was asking for. When you're working on a large, complex idea, people are quick to throw out solutions. But nobody has spent hundreds of hours thinking through every possibility in the way you have. Only the person on the ground, with the dream, can understand all the nuance in the issue. It reminded me of that maxim Neil Gaiman shares with writers: When people tell you something isn't working for them, they're almost always right; when they tell you how to fix it, they're almost always wrong.

But one piece of advice did stick out. "You should connect with Heavy D." I saw that comment almost daily for months and months during my concrete saga. I didn't know a Heavy D from a Heavy C, and I had gone down too many rabbit holes in the previous eight months to give any attention to just a name. But it kept coming up. So finally, I decided to look him up.

I learned "Heavy D" was the nickname of Dave Sparks. A Salt Lake City native, Dave got his start working in construction and on diesel trucks. He posted a few videos online, and that eventually led to a series on the Discovery Channel called *Diesel Brothers,* in which Dave and his best friend Dave Kiley, otherwise known as "Diesel Dave," worked on diesel vehicles in their shop in Utah. Heavy D and Diesel Dave were known for making the impossible happen when it came to vehicles. They were the definition of high-agency people.

The sense, at least online, was that Dave had the resources and mentality to make magic happen.

And as more and more people became invested in the rebuilding of the American Hotel, they thought Dave might be the answer to this nagging concrete problem.

I'd heard more than enough mining myths at that point to be skeptical. Nothing comes easy, and this seemed a bit too easy.

After exchanging a few messages, Dave asked me what problems I was running into at the town. I started off small—there was some wood I was trying to move from a neighboring town. Then a bit more complex—some ore buckets that were stuck on the side of a cliff. Then, as a moonshot, I brought up what I was really struggling with—the eighty yards of concrete that I needed for the footers of the hotel.

"The concrete. That's the most pressing. And it's definitely doable. That's the one." Dave wanted the biggest challenge. That's what he thrives on.

The more impossible it seems, the more he wants to do it. It's a similar feeling to what originally attracted me to Cerro Gordo, to do something hard. Something that tested all of me. Dave had been doing that, specifically related to logistical challenges, for a decade and had the team and machinery to pull it off.

The more time you spend around people who get things done, the more it rubs off on you.

High-agency is contagious. So is the belief that things are figure-out-able.

Figuring out how to get 240,000 pounds of dry concrete, 100,000 pounds of water, and the machinery to mix it all up to Cerro Gordo and into the ground was impossible. Until it wasn't. Heavy D and John Simpson assured me so.

After Edison's factory had burned down, he told reporters he wasn't that worried about it. "I've been through things like this before," he said. He said part of him was happy to be visited by disaster. "It prevents a man from being afflicted with ennui." I have a hard time imagining Heavy D using the word *ennui*. I have a hard time imagining him using the phrase *high-agency* either, but he knew it at his core.

He is homo faber, man the maker. Man, the problem-solver.

"We're going to need an all-wheel-drive mixer truck." Dave called me one night, a few weeks before our big pour. "A couple skid-steers. Excavator. Do you know anyone with a high reach forklift? Wonder if Jax could drive another semi down."

"What are we going to do about the dry mix?" he asked. "Have you figured that out?"

"Yeah, Quikrete down in Corona is willing to mix up some of their supersacks for us. They're one yard each. Weigh three thousand pounds per bag."

"Three thousand pounds?"

"Yeah, each one. We need eighty of them. Seems straightforward." I tried matching Dave's confidence in the conversation.

The process of securing these "supersacks" had been anything but "straightforward." Typically the sacks we were looking for were custom-mixed based on the desired PSI, a measure of the weight it can bear, and the wait time was months. Through some viewers of the channel, I had been put in touch with a guy named Mike, who was another high-agency individual in charge of building runways in remote locations. He was also in charge of most of the concrete work for the Air Force. Because of his pull with the concrete company, we were able to skip the line and get our sacks prepared on time. But their liability ended at the loading bay, meaning it was my responsibility to get 240,000 pounds of concrete from Corona, California—230 miles away—to Keeler, which is as close to the town as they'd go.

"Got it," Dave said. "We'll bring the military trucks, too. How are you getting them to the bottom of the hill?" Dave always thought through each step of a plan twice.

"I have a logistics company out of Riverside bringing them here," I told him.

"Good. Good. If they fall through, let me know. We'll go down and pick them up. You have anything to bring the sacks up the hill?" Dave followed up, mentally tallying how many trips up and down our infamous road would need to be taken to bring up all the bags.

I looked around—the base-model Tacoma I had at the time had a payload capacity of about a thousand pounds. A typical Ford F-150 has a bed capacity of about two thousand pounds. Each one of the eighty sacks we needed to get to town weighed three thousand pounds—about the weight of a brand-new Honda Civic. We needed to move the equivalent of eighty Honda Civics up an eight-mile steep dirt road, in the back of a truck, all without breaking the sacks the concrete was housed in.

"I don't think so," I said. Knowing the real answer was "no."

"All good. We'll sort it out."

Dave was already on to the next item on his mental checklist.

If we were able to get all these sacks to town, the fun would just begin. Each three-thousand-pound sack would have to be lifted approximately twenty feet in the air to be able to be funneled into the hopper of the concrete truck. Cubes of water would have to be hoisted at a similar height. Everything would be mixed together, then the truck would move over to the trenches where the footers were to be poured, pour that mix, and the process would start over again.

"How much water you got up there?" Dave's mental math had shifted to how much water each yard of concrete would need (about thirty gallons a yard, meaning we'd need 2,400 gallons on-site).

"Maybe five hundred, six hundred gallons?" I said, thinking this was a large amount for us to have on hand.

"OK, I'll bring some extra cubes." Dave's list of items he was bringing kept expanding the longer we talked.

"Do we need to rent a bigger backhoe or anything?" I suggested, knowing the small backhoe we had on-site was not going to cut it.

Dave laughed, probably imagining our small backhoe doing all the upcoming work. "Let me figure out the machinery side of it," he said. "You just get the concrete there, the trenches dug, and the rebar in place so we can be ready to pour."

There are people in your life who, when they say they'll handle a certain part of a task, you never quite believe them. Like the kid in grade school who gets added to your group project and on the day you're expecting his contribution, he hasn't even started. Then there are guys like Dave Sparks. When Dave says something will happen on a certain date, that thing will happen on that certain date. Their word is their bond.

I could tell the first time I laid eyes on him that Dave was a man of his word. Just being around him inspired confidence. And it drove me to work even harder.

Once I knew Dave was coming, I was back to life. He was the spark I needed.

I spent hours under headlamps, carefully carving out the trenches of the footers. If this was going to be a group project, I wasn't going to be the kid who didn't do their part.

There's something spiritual about digging in the earth to begin building something that will last far beyond the few short years you have on the planet. It's the old adage about the joy of planting a tree in whose shade you'll never sit. There's a sense of purpose, a sense of worth, that comes from hard labor, and a sense of fulfillment that comes when you know that the fruits of your labor will be enjoyed by people who haven't even been born yet.

This scorched and rocky earth that I was digging was, and I don't use this word lightly, inspiring to me. I was a better man for it. I was putting into practice all the things that Tip had tried to teach me about self-reliance, but with a twist. I was also relying on a team of self-reliant men. I had Dave and his crew at my back. I understood, I mean deeply and truly understood, that this seemingly menial work of digging trenches was something remarkable and it was just the beginning of the skills I'd come to develop during my time here. I was literally digging a new version of myself out of the ashes of the American Hotel. And that reborn me was better than the man I had been before. If we could pull off this absurd feat, what couldn't we pull off? I thought about it over and over sitting inside the backhoe, hyping myself up into a frenzy the day before the pour.

Almost exactly one year after the fire and three weeks after we first spoke, Dave arrived on a blistering June afternoon, looking like he had brought the National Guard with him. His trucks had over-heated coming through Death Valley, where the temperatures were pushing 120 degrees, but he made it in good spirits.

Across four forty-four-foot lowboy trailers pulled by Kenworth heavy-haul semis, Dave brought a six-wheel-drive off-road concrete mixer truck, two decommissioned five-ton military trucks, a CAT 950 loader, a CAT 340 excavator, a skid-steer Bobcat, two four-wheelers, two Ranger side-by-sides, and behind all that, a full-size mobile home. It was a convoy that seemingly stretched a mile along the road. We probably could have taken Baghdad with the equipment mustered there that day, millions of dollars' worth of heavy machinery. But the battalion was here to build rather than destroy.

The night before, I didn't sleep. It still felt too good to be true. After banging my head literally against a concrete wall for so long, it seemed like it was about to be solved.

More than anything else, I felt a sense of camaraderie. Dave brought a dozen of his guys with him—he needed that many to operate all the machines. I had just as many volunteers, some from the local community, others from places far distant, members of the global community of Cerro Gordo. No matter our backgrounds, political beliefs, religions, or anything else, we were all there because we shared a dream of preserving history, and writing it forward. We were necromancers, bent on bringing an old mining town back to life.

On to the task at hand. The logistics of the pour went something like this—the eighty three-thousand-pound bags were delivered by flatbed to Keeler around five A.M. There, each bag was unloaded individually using the Bobcat and then loaded, three at a time, into the beds of the five-ton military trucks. Having two trucks running at all times meant we could haul six bags up the hill at a time. Given the load and the road, each trip took about thirty to forty-five minutes to get up the hill. Given there were eighty bags to get up the hill, the military trucks would be running up and down all day long.

Once the bags were on-site and there were enough to mix in the truck, the CAT excavator would lift up each three-thousand-pound bag, hover it over the hopper of the mixer truck, and dump its contents. In between bags, we would have 250-gallon cubes of water that we would add to the mix. After eight or so bags were dumped in the mixer, we'd drive the mixer over to where the trenches had been made for concrete, and pour. Once poured, the concrete had to be vibrated and smoothed over to ensure that there were no air bubbles in it.

The first few times were rough. The wind was whipping everywhere and concrete dust was burning our eyes. One of the five-ton trucks blew a tire. The loader got a flat tire, too. But slowly, we found our rhythm. The twenty-plus people on-site all found their role and started working as a symphony. Our time between pours went from over an hour to forty-five minutes to thirty minutes.

As the day went on, we all found more energy, even though we had been moving around literal tons of concrete. The plan was working. The American Hotel was rising from the ashes.

I remember at one point chatting with Dave in between pours. We were looking out at all that was being done.

"This has to be one of the best weeks of my life," Dave said, a man who had been pursuing grand adventures for decades.

"It's definitely the best week of mine," I said back. And I meant it.

The day ended under floodlights. We were just pouring the final corner as the sun fully disappeared behind Mt. Whitney. Eighty cubic yards of concrete. Over 300,000 pounds with all the water added, now sitting in the dirt with rebar sticking up, waiting to hold up all my dreams.

Every member of the crew ended the day with a broad smile etched across our dusty, dirty faces. We had accomplished something real. Something tangible. Something that would outlast every one of us. We were, to a man, bone-tired. But I don't know that any of us had ever been happier. I know I hadn't.

As the rest of the crew limped back up to the Gordon House to down some pizza and Gatorades, I was the last man on the concrete. I had a trowel with me and even though the concrete had been pounded and smoothed a dozen times over, I just kept caressing it with my trowel, hunting for any imperfections. It didn't need to be done. Or rather it didn't need to be done for the job to pass muster. But I needed to do it, because I was not yet ready to let go of the joy that this job had given me. I had spent a year mourning the loss of the American, I had spent eight months obsessing over every aspect of this task, and now, I simply wanted to cling to the moment, to the release that came from the work, for as long as I possibly could.

The afterglow of the day was still visible behind the Sierras. I threw the trowel down and sat looking at the silhouette of the mountains, imagining viewing that sunset every night from the porch of the new hotel. Sharing stories and dreams with visitors from all over the world.

Watching each of them fall in love with the view, the history, the magic of this place.

I looked up at all the volunteers and Dave's crew. I thought back to John Simpson. I thought of my future at Cerro Gordo. Nothing is impossible. Nothing ever was. I had the evidence of it cast in eighty cubic yards of concrete.

CHAPTER 12

BURN OUT

A miner spent his days in total darkness, nothing to light his way in the tunnels except the pale weak flame from the lamp fastened to his cap. Every swing of the pick hammered him as hard as it hammered the rock. It sent a shockwave through his body, through his hands, to his elbows and his shoulders. It wasn't an immediate pain. But it was certainly the precursor to pain. And every miner must have known that he only had so many such blows in him. And then there was the sound of the pick against the stone.

Every time the blade hit the stone, it coughed up a cloud of silica dust. It's the most common element on earth, it fills the floor of every ocean, it fills the desert, and down in the mine, the air was thick with it. Every breath a miner took, he was breathing in a million jagged microscopic particles. It got in his eyes and his nostrils. His lungs were filled with it. He must have known that little by little, that dust would turn your lungs to stone.

It's hard to measure out the days of your life when you never see the sun, or never really get to feel the way the breeze shifts from one season to the next up on the surface. And so, instead, he must have measured out his life in fathoms, how deep into the rock he could burrow in the days allotted to him.

If he was worn out, he kept digging. If he was injured, he'd try to work through the pain. If he was crippled, there was another man waiting to take his job. If he was sick and he was lucky, they might have found him a bed in the frontier hospice that a kind soul started down in Lone Pine, where they'd try to comfort him as he coughed up what was left of his lungs. And if he was killed in the hole . . . well, he knew the deal before he ever set foot in this mine.

There were no young men in the mines. By the time a miner was twenty, he had already begun to calcify. By thirty, he was an old man, and if he made it to thirty-five . . .

I'm sitting on the front porch of the Belshaw House. It's my thirty-fifth birthday.

I've been here for three years now, and if you loaded up every hardship and tribulation that I've faced since I arrived into a single mine car and weighed it at the end of the day, it wouldn't amount to half a day's work for one of those old miners.

And yet, I'm weary to the bone.

I almost feel ashamed to say it.

My struggles since I arrived here have been largely of the twenty-first-century variety. The disruption to the global routine that even had consequences here during the pandemic. The angst I went through during a protracted battle with my former partner. Depression. Anxiety. I had appendicitis. But I also had access to health care, and the means to pay for it. There was the blizzard, of course. And the floods. And the fire. Those indeed were existential struggles that the old miners would have recognized. But for the most part, my problems seem almost quaint compared to the daily threats those very old young men faced here.

There are challenges they faced that I can't even imagine. Back in those days, the seething cauldron of vice on the surface made this boomtown every bit as dangerous above ground as it was below. An injudicious comment, a dispute over the price of an ingot of silver, the wrong guy getting the wrong message from the wrong woman at the hotel bar, could, and regularly did, end in bloodshed. At least I've never had to worry about winding up on the wrong end of a derringer or a Colt or a bowie knife.

But still, I'm tired.

And sick. I don't know what's wrong with me. For weeks now, through the entire winter of 2022 and into February of '23, I've been feeling my strength fail, I've been feeling ill. I tried to will my way through it, but I couldn't beat it. It's pronounced enough that even friends of mine on the far side of the country notice it when we talk. My two closest friends threatened to fly out, kidnap me, and drag me off to the closest hospital if I didn't do it myself.

I knew they were right. And that's why I finally drove the four hours to Los Angeles, barely able to keep my head above the steering wheel the whole way. That's why I'm sitting here in this examination room, wearing a humiliating hospital gown, making small talk with the nurse.

"Where are you coming from?" the nurse asks.

"Up on the mountain," I say. "Cerro Gordo."

"You a miner?" she asks.

"Something like that," I say, knowing that the truth is I'm nothing like a miner.

"OK, tell me what's been going on," she says.

Ah, where to begin? Well, there had been three frigid, lonely winters, three blistering summers, and a few biblical storms with wind and rain and dust and snow, sometimes all at once. There had been a woman. There's always a woman. She was as puzzled by my presence in Cerro Gordo as this poor nurse is. Neither one of them understood why I was up there. I don't blame them. It took me a long time to figure it out, too. Then there was a partner, who wouldn't listen. It led to a feud, which led to lawyers. Then there was the mentor, who went to sleep one night and never woke up. All within a year's time.

I want to tell her that I'm lost, that I've been lost more times than I could remember, but this time I felt really lost.

"Any dizziness or falls?" she asks.

"No," I lie. Truth is, I've been falling for years. Metaphorically speaking. And literally. I nearly fell clean off the mountain the very first day I arrived in Cerro Gordo. The last time I fell was while riding a forty-thousand-gallon water tank on the back of a five-ton military surplus six-wheeler. Both on the same stretch of road.

And in between, I'd survived floods that washed away that road, I'd drilled holes in the deep rock in the mines and sucked the silica dust deep into my lungs, I'd accidentally huffed toxic fumes while trying my hand at refining lead ore. And now, I was sick all the time. My head pounded so hard I couldn't sleep, I was nauseous and weak, and every fiber in every muscle and every joint and tendon ached when I moved and when I didn't. And more than anything, I'd lost the desire to do pretty much everything, including getting out of bed each day.

"I've been working a lot," I say.

The doctor comes in. They've run some tests. I don't have pleurisy or consumption or scarlet fever or rickets or any of the other scourges mentioned in all those yellow newspaper clippings from the nineteenth century when they'd note the passing of another young miner.

Irony of ironies, I have a mineral deficiency. Three years in a mining town and it's minerals that I lack.

The doctor and the nurse put their heads together and confer. It's not my diagnosis that baffles them. It's me. Even the documents containing my personal information are confusing and contradictory. My driver's license says I live in Florida, the billing address for my insurance is in Texas, yet my mailing address is a post office box in the middle of the California high desert.

The middle of nowhere.

"How on earth did you end up there?" the doctor asks.

"I don't really know."

"Well, you can't go back up there for a while," the doctor says.

"I have to," I say.

"You can wait a few weeks. You need to rest."

"I can't."

If I didn't get back up to Cerro Gordo soon, I was going to have investors, creditors, bankers after me. But also, I also know something that the doctor doesn't. I know that being away from the mountain for too long would kill me.

This is what Cerro Gordo does to people. It gets in their blood and it never leaves. People who were forced to flee the mountain before they were ready—because of bankruptcy, insanity, threats of violence—always talk about wanting to come back one day. I had seen the words in diaries and letters left behind. They wanted a chance to chase the dream one last time, to see the sunset again, to die up there. Because Cerro Gordo is the only place they ever truly lived.

Everyone who has ever come to Cerro Gordo was looking for something. Silver. Freedom. Fortune. Peace. Anonymity. Themselves. The question is never whether you'll find something there, it's whether you'll find what you're looking for or something else entirely. Whether you'll die before you get it.

The search itself is elemental. It is fundamental to the human impulse for exploration. It defines the spirit of the adventurer.

I am no exception. I came looking for a lot of things. A challenge. Fulfillment. Purpose. A different way to be. I found some of them. Some remained elusive. Other things I wasn't looking for, but I found when I most desperately needed them.

The doctor tells me that it's fortunate I came in when I did. If I'd waited much longer, I risked long-term damage.

"People can die from this, you know."

"They can die from a lot worse."

He pretended he didn't hear.

But it's true. Despair will kill you as surely as cirrhosis. The richest man in the graveyard is still dead. And he probably died wishing for something. It's the wishing that kills you.

It's the following morning. I'm checking out, and the charge nurse is making small talk as he reviews my paperwork.

"Cerro Gordo, huh? That old ghost town?"

"Yep."

"What are you doing up there?"

"I love it there."

"Why?"

And for the first time in the few years that I'd lived at Cerro Gordo, I didn't have a firm answer for him. My enthusiasm had waned, my unwavering vision was blurred. I was having a harder and harder time understanding why I was spending my time on a town that had a reputation only for grinding people and mountains to dust.

What was it all for?

Everything seemed to be turning on me. The things that I originally enjoyed now gave me little or no joy at all. I had become especially anxious about posting videos. Anxious all the time. When I started the YouTube channel, I didn't understand that I was signing a contract. A contract that if the channel were to be successful, I'd get lots of support. But in exchange I'd need to produce or reap the consequences of not doing so. When I posted the video about the fire, I had done so hoping to find understanding and support. The support had come. Way, way, way more support than I could have ever imagined.

In the time since the demands on me have grown exponentially, I've dealt with stalkers on several occasions. Death threats. Strange things sent to me in the mail. People who showed up, literally on my front doorstep, and said, "I came here to die." I had people email me their intentions to kill themselves if I didn't write back. Every private moment has become public. It started to feel in my low moments that I am a character in a show. *The Truman Show*, but unable to show my truly dark moments. It's not what people want. It's not my character. Social media is a delicate balance of needs.

I guess I had gotten a taste of celebrity. And I just didn't want it. Or like anyone new to having a public personality, I wished it to be on terms I could control. But that's hard to do. What started off as an exciting experience had blossomed into something requiring full-time employees, countless contractors, dozens of volunteers on a weekly basis, hundreds of visitors on busy weekends, and many many people online impatiently awaiting the next video. All wanting more than I had to give. I was trying to find the balance between my marketing day job (which paid the bills for the town), creating new videos for the huge online community, keeping the projects in the town going, playing general contractor on a commercial hotel re-build, managing the staff and the volunteers, and greeting the hundreds of people who were now coming up to Cerro Gordo. It was all too much. I was burned out.

I have become that candle in Edna St Vincent Millay's poem:
My candle burns at both ends;
It will not last the night;
But ah, my foes, and oh, my friends—
It gives a lovely light!

"Burnout" is such a twenty-first-century term. We toss it around so casually. The slightest fatigue, the angst and ennui of modern life, we chalk it all up to burnout. We've cheapened the phrase.

We forget that not so terribly long ago it had a very specific meaning. The term *burnout* was coined by a German American psychologist named Herbert J. Freudenberger in the 1970s to describe the "physical or mental collapse caused by overwork or stress."

Freudenberger was working as a psychiatrist at St. Mark's Free Clinic in New York's East Village in between his private practice work. He and a group of volunteers were consulting with drug addicts and the homeless. Working long hours, he eventually observed that he and his fellow volunteers were increasingly emotionally depleted and tired of the work.

After many requests from friends and family, Freudenberger agreed to go on vacation. Cramming in work the night before, he couldn't get out of bed and missed the flight the next morning.

Trying to make sense of the experience, he recorded himself talking about it, and when he played the tape back, he was taken aback by the anger and exhaustion he could hear in his own voice.

He summarized his observations from the recording and among his coworkers in his 1974 paper "Staff Burn-Out," borrowing the term from the drug addicts he was working with, but also likening it to raging fires that literally exhaust themselves in their fury.

As Freudenberger put it: "As a practicing psychoanalyst, I have come to realize that people, as well as buildings, sometimes burn out. Under the strain of living in our complex world, their inner resources are consumed as if by fire, leaving a great emptiness inside, although their outer shells may be more or less unchanged . . . Only if you venture inside will you be struck by the full force of the desolation."

In the twenty-four months since I publicly vowed to rebuild the hotel, I could literally feel my passion for the project consuming me. The fire that swallowed the American Hotel was still raging long after the last living embers had been doused— it was burning inside me, turning my will to ash.

Like Freudenberger, my friends, too, had been begging me for months to take a vacation. I couldn't hear their pleas over the roaring of the fire.

And just like Freudenberger, I had been recording myself, and in the more recent recordings, I was concerned with what I was hearing. I had lost weight, a lot of weight. I wasn't taking care of myself. I was putting absolutely everything in front of any of my basic needs. Sometimes when I rewatched a video, I'd barely recognize myself. Mentally, physically, and spiritually, I was self-immolating. Like Freudenberger, I knew something had to change.

That's what led me into the hospital. But what led me to change wasn't the warnings of the medical professionals. It wasn't even my concerned friends calling. It was a book I happened to pick up a few days after the doctors warned me that people had died from situations similar to mine.

The book was about World War II. It was on a dusty shelf in the Belshaw House. Flipping through it one time, I found a section about the rotations that soldiers went through when they were on the front line. The book made the argument that the single most important issue for troops in combat situations was how often soldiers were permitted to leave the front line. In the British Army, the rotations were typically sixteen days. Each soldier usually spent eight days on the front line, four days in the reserve trench, and then four days in a rest camp set far enough back from the fighting to give the soldiers time to revive themselves. Too many days on the front line, soldiers became useless. Constant stress, with no relief, is as deadly as a bullet on a battlefield.

I am not comparing my day-to-day struggles to the horrors faced by soldiers on the front lines of any war. I'm not yet insane. But the idea of a rotation stuck with me. I needed to get off the mountain. I knew this fact for a long time, but the idea of it terrified me. I was afraid that I would lose momentum, that one day would be one week, and that eventually, I'd just never come back. That Cerro Gordo would once again be abandoned. I had given my word that I would never do that, and so here I was, white-knuckling my way through the day, and then through the next day and the day after that. Who would manage my obligation in my absence? Who would direct the contractors for the hotel, and the volunteers who had come from all over to help? I loved Cerro Gordo. But after two years, it felt like a prison of my own making.

I thought about the portrait of Mortimer Belshaw that hung above the shelf where I had found the book. I wondered if he felt the same oppressive weight on his shoulders while he was up here. If he ever felt trapped in his own town. Or did he implement a "rotation" where he occasionally went off the hill? Perhaps. History tells us that he built himself a lovely home in Lone Pine, and another in Bakersfield, refuges from the grinding demands of the mining camp.

And then I was back on the mountain, not at all restored after my visit to the doctor. Looking out the window, I stared at the Gordon House. There, too, perhaps, was a clue to finding the balance between work and rest. There's no doubt that Louis D. Gordon, "LD" as he was known, was a restless man. He was the man responsible for finding zinc here in 1910. Long after the silver vein was lost and everyone had packed up and left, LD came and discovered zinc in the waste left behind. That discovery would lead to another twenty years of prosperity for Cerro Gordo as it quickly became the largest zinc supplier in the United States. LD was known to be a very hands-on owner. Unlike Belshaw, Gordon would go into the mine every day to see how progress was coming along. There are photos of him helping repair broken windows. He was responsible for putting up the aerial tramway that extended from the town down eight miles to Keeler, saving his operation from having to send ore down Belshaw's Yellow Grade Road. There is a framed photo in his house of him riding inside one of the ore buckets on its return trip back up the cable tramway. He's smoking a cigar, smiling and waving as he rides a potential deathtrap.

He built the house I was staring at in 1912. It's much larger than Belshaw's house. It's much more refined in ways that can't just be attributed to the forty-year gap between construction. It was built with the hopes of persuading his wife, Cornelia, to move to the mining town with him. LD and Cornelia had married long before LD discovered his riches in the waste rock at Cerro Gordo. LD was passionate about Cerro Gordo, but he also loved his wife. He knew mining camps were not the most appealing choice of locations for women of the day, so he set out to build the most accommodating home he could. As legend goes, Cornelia came up, spent a few weeks at the town, and left. She much preferred, needed even, the comforts and social life of a "real" town. So LD, for the rest of his life, split his time between this mining camp and Cornelia's comfortable home in the world outside of Cerro Gordo.

None of the previous owners of Cerro Gordo had spent 100 percent of their time on the hill. They had rotations of their own. Ways to allow some of the pressure out of the cooker of being there. It was the only way they were able to achieve such impressive feats as they did on the hill.

Wandering to my bathroom mirror, seeing a shadow of myself looking back, I knew I had to leave. It felt selfish, but I came to understand that this wasn't just for me, it was for everyone who was counting on me. If I stayed here and drove myself to the point of collapse, then the whole project I had undertaken here would collapse with me. Even if it was just a few days a month, I needed distance from Cerro Gordo, and Cerro Gordo needed me to take the time to restore myself.

I would die if I stayed away from Cerro Gordo too long. That's what I had told the doctor. And it was absolutely true. But I would also die if I allowed Cerro Gordo to hold me as a hostage.

And so, at last, I left the mountain. It was around the holidays, so I decided to drive to Vegas, catch a plane home, and see my parents. I remember that the entire four-hour drive to Las Vegas, all I wanted to do was turn right back around. But I pushed through, and for the first time in nearly two years, I was off the mountain for more than a day or two.

On the flight home, I felt a bit like Tom Hanks in *Cast Away*. My beard was long and scraggly; my hair hadn't been properly cut in years. I remember playing with the faucet in the airplane lavatory, fascinated by the notion that this flying bus at 35,000 feet had running water and yet in my house, I rarely did. The gods must be crazy here.

When I first came to Cerro Gordo, I remember a distinct "hump" that happened around my third day here. The first three days you are acutely aware of how, well, gross, it can be not showering regularly. Not having the amenities that most take for granted. Then, by the third day, you've accepted your filthy fate and looked beyond it to all the amazing things around you. I found that on the other end of a stint here, it would take a similar number of days to readjust to the "normal" world once you were back in it. The fact that the water just turned on. The idea that you were expected to shower, to go see people at the end of the day. I wondered if it would take me years to re-adjust.

I spent more time in the shower at my parents' home than I care to admit. Several times a day, I just stood there, basking in the spray. I'd towel off, and then off I'd go. I reconnected with high school friends. I went diving and played golf. Golf. What a ridiculously civilized game. A decadent waste of land and iron. And I relished every moment of it.

For the first time in years, I was living in a world not marked by hardship and deprivation, a world where I wasn't figuring everything out by the seat of my pants, a world where there were people who cared about me. I felt safe. I felt the weight being lifted off of my back. I felt myself being restored.

It may sound like hyperbole, but I honestly believe that trip may have saved my life. 1 had lost thirty pounds my first year on the mountain. As someone who has always worn a belt on the smallest hole, I did not have thirty pounds to lose. In those intermittent moments on the mountain when I did sleep, I slept like the dead. But I was also dead tired every day. I got strong the way miners and farmers always do—I probably could have crushed a walnut with my bare hands if I could have found one, and my back was strong enough that I could probably have pulled off a Big Bad John with a mine timber if the need arose. But I was getting weak in other ways. My joints were killing me. I don't want to think about the kind of vitamin deficiencies I was walking around with. The nearest fresh vegetable was probably still growing in the farmland of the Central Valley on the other side of the Sierras across the valley from me. And that asparagus had already been promised to the buyers at Kroger's or Whole Foods.

These were just things I lived with. They were facts of life on the mountain and part of the reality of bringing Cerro Gordo back to life. It's only upon reflection, with some distance, that I can see the irony of it all. That in trying to bring a town back to life I was jeopardizing my own life.

But that's what happens when you have a fire in your gut, an all-consuming passion. It consumes all. Even you.

There are minefields in a mining town like Cerro Gordo. Step wrong and you can lose your money. No big deal. You can always make more. Trip and you might lose a friend. Again, so what? If you can lose a friend that easily, maybe they weren't really your friend in the first place.

But take one really false step, and you can lose yourself. And that, you'll never recover from. That's the thing about mines and minefields. You never know which step is a step too far.

It is so easy to lose yourself inside a big dream. It can happen so fast. Because it's all you think about. We see this with entrepreneurs, artists, and musicians all the time. It feels like almost without exception you could pick the name of a famous founder or a master painter or a musical virtuoso out of a hat, and if you were able to find a picture of them from before all their success, when they were younger and fully in the paroxysms of obsession, you'd see how truly lost they were. It's etched on their flesh, in their thinning hair and graying skin, bags under the eyes; it manifests itself in addiction, insomnia, mania, paranoia. These are the wages of obsession.

Sometimes, what we do for work is fundamentally not normal. It takes those circumstances to do something great. But you must be aware of the place, mentally, physically, that we go to in order to do that.

It's a cruel paradox. It's only when you find something that matters as much to you as your obsession, something that balances it and puts it in perspective, that you can truly achieve your dreams.

Maybe it's philanthropy, or starting a family, or having a hobby, or finding God. Whatever it takes, who am I to judge? There must be something outside of your dreams to make those dreams a reality. In a way it's like building a fire. There must be room for the air to flow or the fire will die.

Personally, losing myself inside big projects has always been way too easy, because I think about them all as adventures, and half the point of an adventure is to get sufficiently lost so that you have fresh eyes to find whatever it is you're looking for. I realize now that it was preordained that I would risk losing myself in Cerro Gordo. It's the way I was always wired. It's what I asked for. An adventure that spans both space and time. Hundreds of acres in every direction and hundreds of years into the past. Thousands of feet above sea level and thousands of feet underground. A massive four-dimensional living puzzle that is, by its nature, not fully knowable, no matter how much I want to know it all, no matter how obsessed I am with solving it.

I'm back at Cerro Gordo. I'm stronger now. Healthier. I'm still driven by the dream of making Cerro Gordo thrive again. But I no longer think of it as bringing Cerro Gordo back. I treasure what Cerro Gordo once was; every token of its past is a kind of holy relic to me. But I do not want to make it what it was before. What it was before was a town built on extraction, on the notion that you take everything of value and then leave the ruins behind. That ethos was so deeply engrained in the place that the place itself did to the miners what the miners did to Cerro Gordo. It took everything from them and left nothing behind. It did it to them, it did it to me. I never

AIR

There is no such thing as silence. Even the subtlest movement by the smallest creature disturbs the air that surrounds it and carries the sound of that disturbance as far as the wind will take it. There's a rhythm to the flapping of a butterfly's wings, a song. You may not be able to hear it, but it's there. The percussion of your own heartbeat, the counterpoint of your own breath—the world was not built to allow any of us to move through it silently. The air that surrounds us demands that we each make a sound. It cannot be avoided. I don't believe I ever really understood that until I moved to Cerro Gordo. In fact, it took me quite a while after I arrived that I realized it. Coming from a bustling city like Austin, at first I had mistaken solitude for silence. But then one day, high enough on the hill that the air was clear and thin, a place where I could see for miles, it dawned on me that every living thing that moves through the air has a song to sing, a story to tell, and even when nothing stirs, the breeze itself will sigh.

On bad days, I think wind exists solely to remind you that things can always get worse. It's the unwelcome alarm clock whistling through the 150-year-old planks assembled into the house I'm sleeping in. It screeches as it moves through the sage grass and the few remaining pinyon pines, before it slams up against the house like a car accident. The sound of the corrugated metal tacked to the eaves bending under its strain; of unsecured items pinballing through town on a journey to nowhere. These signal to me that the wind is really howling and that I should steel myself against it.

And then I remind myself that the air is just doing what it does. It's neither good nor bad. It's my perception of what is going on around me.

There's no way you can come to a place like Cerro Gordo and not make a sound. The sound you make, whether it's a psalm or a sorrowful dirge, that's entirely up to you.

CHAPTER 13

SEEK AWE

It begins before dawn most mornings. A kind of yearning. Anticipation stronger than any alarm. Turning over in my bed, all is still black outside. The moon has waned.

The stars have retreated. And I'll take a small comfort in the knowledge that I have not missed it.

I'll stumble from my bed, toss on yesterday's clothes, fumble with boots still stiff from the night's chill. It's not always easy. Sometimes my body, stiff as my boots, resists. Sometimes my soul does. Some mornings I have to force myself. Especially on the coldest mornings.

My destination is a rock outcropping high on the northern peak of the property. A spot from which I can scan the entire horizon. There are, of course, spots like this all over the world, places where in the solitude of a vista, you can, if you're still, observe the miracles that happen every day.

The rock atop the Temple Mount where Abraham is said to have almost sacrificed Isaac, and where Mohammed, it is said, ended his journey around the globe in a single night is now imprisoned within the confines of a magnificent jail made of marble and tile. In the Black Hills in South Dakota, hemmed in now by manicured trails, the most sacred rock in all that expanse has been vandalized, chiseled into a monument to our national vanity that you can only observe from below. We celebrate such places for their holiness and then punish them for the unpardonable sin of being holy, for reminding us that we are only a small part of the ongoing daily miracle of creation.

For my part, I'll leave this place the way it's been since the beginning of time. And every morning, I'll make my way up here, either on foot or on my motorcycle. To be honest, these days, I usually take the bike. The road I ride up here is strewn with shale and gravel, sharp shards of stone chipped out of the earth and dumped by the miners of the last century and the century before that. The miners are all gone. The road remains.

When I reach that rock at the crest of the hill, I'll sit or stand in silence, and watch as the first gentle wave of light breaks over on the horizon, then marvel as bands of color, red and golden, announce the rising of the sun over Death Valley. And at the end of the day, weary and covered with the grime of a full day's work, I'll return here, face westward, and watch as the sun turns its face from the world.

I wish I could tell you that the place is pristine, untouched, that our species has never tried to build a wall or a fence around it, never tried to shackle the miracle. I can't. Indeed, there is a fence and a gate. I share the key with the bureaucrats in the Federal Aviation Administration. I have no idea what they do out there in the desert. I don't ask and they don't say. We're less than a hundred miles from Area 51. Is there a connection? Not wanting to share this place with any more people than I already have to, I choose not to speculate.

I'm a bit ashamed of my selfishness, but I've actually come to be grateful for that gate. It guarantees that my daily ritual will be mine alone. I've come to regard the heavy metallic groan of the gate as it opens as part of the ritual, a kyrie chanted by a chorus at the beginning of my daily devotion. Sometimes, the gate will get ahead of me as I open it, swinging back and slamming against the rock wall into which it's been cut with a chest-pounding clang and then two or three more softer clangs as it bounces once or twice against the rock.

Next on my twice-daily pilgrimage to the rock, I navigate a stretch of dirt road that clings precariously to the side of a cliff. Sometimes, on the days when I'm feeling particularly generous with my solitude, I'll bring a friend or two along. They always hate this part of the journey. A false step, they fear, and they would plummet over the side to almost certain death.

I had those same fears myself, in the beginning. Now I've learned to look forward, toward those distant snow-capped peaks of the Sierras, the place where Muir famously lost his mind and found his soul.

And finally, I'm there, this private place out in the open, some fifty feet below the top of the ridge, this rock of mine that almost seems to be floating.

I have no idea how this rock came to stand where it does.

Maybe it slid down there many years ago and decided, as I have, that this is precisely where it needs to be. It will not budge. The shale around it moves with the slightest touch, but the boulder stays in place. There's a lesson in that, too, I suppose.

Sitting on the rock you can see the jagged peak of Mt. Whitney above the clouds to the west and the vast desert of Death Valley, literally miles below, to the east. From here you can see the highest and lowest points in the continental United States, a day's walk from each other, but up here both are caught in a single gaze. I can see the frigid mountain tops where the air is too thin for a man to breathe easily, and in the same glance the broiling desert where the hot wind scorches your lungs. A study in contrasts, in extremes, a humbling revelation of the yin and the yang.

Most days when I make it up here, the wind is still. The heat of the day has not yet warmed the air enough for its currents to start contending with each other. The tumbleweed waits impatiently for the inevitable breeze to come and move it along its way. The junipers hold on to their precious, fragile berries, knowing that before the day ends, some of them will be shaken to the ground. Rub them between your thumb and forefinger, and their juice smells like gin. It's intoxicating. Everything up here is.

It's the first moment of the first day of the world, and it comes every single day.

A writer I know, who grew up in a rural community surrounded by hard-shell Christian fundamentalists, once wrote that he felt sorry for those people who were bound by their rigid interpretation of scripture to believe that the world was created in seven days some four thousand years ago, because that blinded them to the ongoing miracle of creation unfolding across every day of their lives.

Up here, I understand what he meant. On those stillest of mornings, I can hear my own heartbeat, and feel that I am a part of the very act of bringing being into being.

Sometimes a sound will intrude on the stillness. I'll hear something in the distance moving through the shale. It's nothing big, I know that. Larger animals rarely venture up this high—there's too little water, too little cover for them. This is the domain of the lesser creatures, the jackrabbits and the chipmunks. The rustling as they move through the stone is not a disturbance, as I first thought. It's a gift from the silence. Only here is it so quiet that you can hear the footfalls of a chipmunk, the least amongst us, from a hundred yards away.

Up here, at nine thousand feet above sea level, the air is so thin that the slightest movement ripples through it like a summer breeze through a bed sheet on a clothesline, carrying even the smallest sound far farther than it would in the soupy air down below.

There is a story that old desert wanderers used to tell about the Prophet Elijah, how he could not find the voice of the divine in the roaring thunder or the crashing of the sea in a storm, but found it instead as a still, small voice, a whisper in a desert cave. Up here I understand what they meant.

We use the word "awe" and imagine that it must roll in on thunder. In truth, when we find it, it's often in silences.

We are often so far removed from awe that even the word has become meaningless, degraded to the point that we use it to describe the most pointless and meaningless things. It's become a filler word, used to respond when we're not really paying attention. No matter how many times we say it, the story we're responding to is probably not "awesome." But silence can be.

The sights, the silence, the way the stillness amplifies and ennobles every footfall and heartbeat, this is, I believe, the first place I've been where I have ever truly experienced awe. You can lose yourself in the awe of the place. Or you can find yourself. But what if that's the wrong way of looking at it? Maybe that's a vestige of my decidedly First World upbringing, this notion that I must interpret the world that stretches out before me up here through the prism of my own sense of self. What can this place give to me? Isn't that just a slightly less rapacious version of the same thing that drove Mulholland to loot the lakebed?

There it is, take it.

Maybe, instead, I need to learn how to just be, and just be here. This vista would exist without me, the conversation between the desert floor and the mountaintop, the way the clouds and the shadows play across the horizon. There would be an act of creation this morning, whether I was present or not. But without my heartbeat, without that scurrying chipmunk, it would not be this act of creation. If there's one thing I've found in the letters and papers of Cerro Gordo residents across the last 160 years, it's the recognition of the power and nature of this place. It intimidated some of them. It inspired others. It made yet others question the meaning of things. But we all got up with the sun, put in a full day's work, and wound down our day with the sun. And that has been oddly calming to me. It's made the hard stuff easier, and the easy stuff feels like a gift.

Coming back from the doctor, returning from my medically mandated break in Florida, I was still grappling with the aftermath of two tumultuous years. My relationship with the town was not in danger of being torn apart—we weren't heading for a divorce—but we were in trouble . . . and friends were beginning to whisper about us.

The crises I had faced here hadn't gone away when I had. I had sedated myself with the numbing comforts of what we call the "real world" of manicured golf courses and strip malls in Florida. I had taken a "vacation" in some real estate agent's fantasy, where I was the center of the universe. The mountains and the desert and the work yet to be done in Cerro Gordo never even noticed that I was gone. As most of the 350 million of us in my urban and suburban tribe are, I'm petty enough that I took their indifference to my presence personally. More than once upon my return, coping with the relentless cold, and the lack of running water and the lack of flowing capital, and the disappearing contractors, I found myself pining for the narcotic comfort of that fake "real world."

I did my best to combat my restlessness and resentment by plunging headfirst back into the work at hand. That basically meant that I was plunging headfirst into a pile of cinderblocks that had not, in my absence, miraculously transformed themselves into the foundation for the hotel.

Turned out that the contractor I had hired before I left had decided to take a bit of a vacation himself.

No big deal, I thought. I'll just lay them myself. That's when I discovered that the missing contractor had ordered the wrong kind of blocks. I would have to order new ones, and there was no telling how long it might be before they were delivered.

Looking back, I realize that that particular snafu was actually the high point of a day that spiraled nose-first into absurdity from there.

It reached its pinnacle when a large, bearded man driving an equally large van pulled up outside my house, stalked to the front door, banged on it loudly and incessantly, and when I failed to answer in what he deemed to be a timely fashion, he plunked himself down on my porch and waited. You got the sense that the guy would still be there today if I hadn't by chance had to dash to the outhouse and caught a glimpse of him along the way.

I don't think I had even had a chance to say hello before the bearded man launched into a long and expletive-riddled oration about how the whole world was fucked and how he planned to escape to Cerro Gordo to get away from it all, how he and his buddy could turn the place into an armed camp where the chosen could spend the end times fighting off the globalist hordes that would surely descend on him and his embattled remnant. It took me fifteen minutes to crowbar my way out of that very one-sided conversation.

I wish I could tell you that was the only time I had ever had such a conversation in Cerro Gordo. It wasn't. There are far too many people in America who, when faced with the silent solitude of deserted places, fearfully fill that silence with their own very loud delusions.

With the words of the zombie Thomas Paine still echoing in my head, I stumbled into the cabin and opened my computer. The first thing I saw was an angry missive from a disgruntled fan, a person who had made the trek to Cerro Gordo and was disappointed—no, furious—that I had not been there. Apparently, that was enough of an affront that this person had made it their personal mission in life to warn everyone in the entire universe that I was a miserable human being.

I was still stewing over that email when my phone rang. It was our architect, who cheerfully told me that his office had made a minor mistake while drafting the plans for the hotel. Well, not minor, actually. The plans had to be completely redrafted, and oh, by the way, we were going to need a lot more concrete, a lot more money, and the whole thing was going to take a lot more time.

Ego. Vanity. Anger and ineptitude. It's a contagion that thrives in the lower elevations and sometimes it makes it up here. But it can't survive above the tree line. I leave the troubling screen and pick back up my trowel and return to work, but soon enough, I cast my gaze toward the mountaintops. The sun is starting its descent. I hold up my hand and measure the distance between the sun and the horizon. Two fingers. Thirty minutes.

"The mountains are calling, and I must go." As is read on the back of every Jeep in the Sierras.

It's five minutes of peace as I flog my motorcycle up the gravel road to the gate, then through it.

Along the way, I soak in the rugged beauty of the weathered wood on the buildings in town, and revel in the way the sagebrush near the museum shivers in the breeze. From my saddle, I spot tracks, paw prints leading downhill from the old cemetery, too big to be a feral cat, too small to be a mountain lion. I have no idea what left those tracks. I'm content with the mystery. A bit farther on, a pinyon tree has fallen and blocked the road. No problem; I'll simply go around it. Farther along, there's a small round rock, the size of a softball, sunning itself in the road. It wasn't there this morning. I don't know what caused that rock to roll there. Mountains move, one stone at a time. On the other side of the continent, the Appalachians were once the tallest mountains in the world, taller than the Rockies, taller than the Andes, but one stone at a time they rolled away, until now they're just a pile of rocks where the mountains used to be. The ongoing miracle of creation is also a miracle of destruction. Someday, in the far, far distant future, these mountains will tumble and the valley will be filled. But not today. Not for a million years.

It's golden hour when I reach my rock, that perfect moment

when the sinking sun casts everything in argent. Sometimes, when the air is still and the light just right, it feels like you're trapped in amber. No. Not trapped. Held. But just for a heartbeat.

I stare directly across at Mt. Whitney's snow-capped peak. It feels like it's alive and I wonder if the mountain notices me. Behind it, shafts of gold, fingers of light, rise into the blueness of the sky, as if the sun is trying to cling to the last instant of the day.

Twice a day for three years, and still I'm humbled—and proud—to be part of this wonder. The mountains and the sky and the valley and the setting sun, the man with the beard and the architect and the disappointed traveler from my computer, we're all connected. By place, by time, by desire.

The Stoics had a term for this sense of place and interconnectedness. They call it *sympatheia*. It's the idea of mutual interdependence, that we're all woven together in the tapestry of existence and must look after each other. *Mundus ipse est ingens deorum omnium templum* ("The world itself is a huge temple of all the gods"), as Seneca would say.

Take me to church.

I feel small, smaller than the chipmunk that scurries through the shale. And I feel gigantic, as massive as the miracle that plays out every day before my eyes.

It's no wonder that monumental, awe-inspiring places like Owens Valley and the Inyo Mountains are so often called God's country. They were—they are—present for the creation, they're present for the destruction. They'll always be here in some form or another.

And so will I.

CHAPTER 14

GRATITUDE

My poor truck was never meant to carry such a heavy load. It says so right there on the warning sign in the glove box. What the hell. We all carry burdens heavier than we're meant to.

It's been a year since Heavy D and his boys rode in like the cavalry with cement mixers and poured eighty yards of concrete to set the footers of the hotel. A year. It feels like a thousand, and still we're not done. We're not at the end. We're not at the beginning of the end. We're not even at the end of the beginning. There are still a few tons of concrete to be poured to finish the foundation, and until that's done, we're dead in the water. Or would be if we had any water.

There's a storm brewing this weekend. If we don't pour that remaining concrete now, we'll have to wait until the winter weather passes and it becomes warm enough for the concrete to flow.

That's six months, easily.

And so, once again, I'm racing against time and the elements, my own limitations and the fussy limitations of my old truck. My poor truck was never meant to carry such a heavy load. Welcome to the club.

There's four thousand pounds of concrete packed into my truck bed. That asthmatic straight-six is having a seizure as I flog it up the Yellow Grade Road. Even under normal circumstances the engine groans and mutters curses going up that road. Now it's howling in anguish, and the dash is lit up like Macy's Christmas display, furiously, frantically flashing warning lights at me in runic code, yellow and red and—what the hell does that one mean?

If my old truck were a horse, the merciful thing would be to shoot her. My truck's too young to be this old. So am I.

There are two other four-wheel-drive trucks right behind me, and they're struggling just as much as mine is. And right behind them, is a guy we just call D and his truck—a two-wheel-drive, poor guy. We only gave him half a load.

I'm not the first in line. Right in front of me is the lead vehicle in our dismal convoy, a military five-ton carrying twelve thousand pounds of concrete. Dave Sparks had left the truck behind and it's a beast. We've hauled ten tons in it, but this is the biggest load we've ever asked it to bear. I'm optimistic.

Keep it slow, real slow, and it'll make it. I hope.

All the way up the eight-mile torture track we're one burnt valve away from disaster. And once we get to the top, we're just getting started. Somebody's going to have to help us unload all 36,000 pounds of concrete, 1,500 bags of it; somebody's gonna have to help us cut them open and mix the concrete with what little water we have, muscle the concrete up twelve feet and pour it inside the cinderblocks that we have stacked for the foundation. Then, and only then, will we have reached the end of the beginning of the project to rebuild the American Hotel.

I'm always reluctant to ask for help. But this weekend, I'm desperate. I'm also deeply gratified that so many people, volunteers like Hans and Elliot and D, guys who were until recently strangers, have put themselves and their trucks in harm's way to help me this weekend.

I'm grateful. I'm humbled.

Funny, they never mention that in the blueprints or the materials list. Gratitude. Humility. They're as critical as concrete in a project like this. They're the things that bind the individuals in a team together the way concrete cements the blocks in the foundation.

I've learned a lot about gratitude and humility since Heavy D first came to the mountain. He taught me that every task was manageable, that no problem was too big, that everything was "figure-out-able" as long as you could appeal to people who had that figure-it-out gene imprinted on their DNA. And you could appeal to them if you respected them and allowed yourself to be humbled by their talents and skills, and as long as you were truly grateful, not for just what they did, but for who they are.

The concrete, the basement, is getting done this weekend.

The stage was set last night. Twenty or so of us had been up past sunset preparing.

Almost every one of the twenty people on-site had been to the town over the past two years and volunteered their time. They were no longer going to town to meet me, or tour the property. They were there because the love of Cerro Gordo had gotten into their blood. They'd made friends.

They'd fallen under the same spell of the town that I had. They were emotionally invested in seeing this town come back to life. And we all understood that finally finishing off the basement was the pivot point on which the rest of the whole dream was balanced. We couldn't wait to begin.

We were going to pull off the impossible, and this time we were going to do it ourselves.

The plan was complex and needed to be executed within a weekend. People had to return home. Equipment on loan needed to be returned.

We had, with much anxiety and distress, accomplished the first step. The concrete was now on-site. Now we turned our sights on mixing it. Each bag had to be cut open and emptied into the bucket of our Kubota skid-steer. Once the bucket was full, the skid-steer would bring the dry mix over to the auger, which was essentially a funnel to get the concrete into the mixer. Above the auger was a hopper that our neighbor Aaron had jury-rigged himself. The figure-out-able had been figured out. Water would be added, dry mix would become wet cement, and hopefully we'd end up with a half yard or yard of concrete. We weren't yet sure how much we could fit in.

Once the concrete was wet, the clock was ticking. We then needed to get the mixed concrete out of the mixer and into the walls before it started to harden.

That involved pouring the concrete into a giant metal bucket that had a horizontal slit at the bottom. The concrete would go into the bucket, then be lifted over the wall with our mini excavator, where someone would pull the handle, releasing the contents of the bucket inside the cells of the cinder blocks making up the wall. All at a dead run.

Nothing to it. Rinse and repeat. Something like fifty times.

There were issues throughout this plan. First, our mini excavator did not have a long enough arm to lift the bucket the fifteen feet or so it needed to get above the wall with room for the bucket underneath.

After scratching our heads for a few hours, trying longer chains, etc., I realized the answer was sitting right in front of us—the five-ton military truck. The bed of the truck sits about six feet off the ground. If we were to put the mini excavator in the bed of the truck, then that should give us just enough room. The crowd was split on this idea. The idea of having the tiny mini excavator lifting thousands of pounds from below it and reaching it over the wall gave some people some pause.

As the owner of the town (and operator of the mini excavator) I made an executive decision and started building a dirt berm that would act as a loading bay to get the excavator into the truck. We backed the truck up to the side of the berm, I moved dirt to cover a gap between the end of the bed and the edge of the berm, and it was time. The excavator swayed and bumped as I backed it into the bed of the truck just as the sun was turning everything pink. I sat in the excavator, looking backward toward the mountains and the setting sun as our town manager Scotty drove the five-ton as close as he could to the basement wall. The added six feet of clearance would give us just enough space to get the bucket over the wall. Since we had to use the five-ton in the morning to move a few more pallets, the actual test would have to be a game-day consideration.

Driving up, I acknowledged to myself that I, too, had a few doubts about this part of the plan. The excavator could be too weak to lift the full bucket. The weight of the bucket could tip over the excavator.

A chain could break. The mixer could stop working. The weather could . . .

"Enough," I told myself. The volunteers were waiting for the concrete to arrive and for me to give the final marching orders for the day. To begin what we all understood was to be a historic day.

It's strange knowing that a dozen or so people, most of whom are older than me, were waiting for me to give the order. I'd not thought of myself as a leader. In past jobs I gravitated to things I could do on my own. If I had to be part of a team, I was not one of those peak performance guys who subscribes to "iron sharpening iron." I wanted everyone to be on the same page and, when possible, to write that page together. But that doesn't always work when you have a big goal, limited resources, and a ticking clock. As the author of your own dream, you are in a leadership role by default, and when people show up for your dream, it will always be up to you to tell them what role they can play. Even when it's not your first instinct, you must take ownership of your authority and accept that it's your job to push, to drive, to guide. But you must also give the full measure of respect to the sacrifice others have made to embrace your dream.

As our convoy crept into town, the first light of day was creeping across the Owens Valley, casting everything in an odd purple hue—even the Carhartts and coveralls that a few of the volunteers had donned to prepare themselves for a brutal day of manual labor seemed to me to be tinged with a purple glow, the ancient color of nobility. Appropriate, I thought.

They were gathered together in a tight circle at the edge of the worksite, as if they were trying to conserve their heat. They clutched steaming coffee cups and shuffled their feet to shake off the needles of the piercing cold. They should have been miserable. But they weren't. There was joy in the tight circle, and excitement. Once again, I felt it. That gratitude. That humility.

I was in their hands. Cerro Gordo was in their hands. And they were good hands. We were being taken care of. The guys, the volunteers, weren't just helping me get the American Hotel over the line, they were carrying me across the line, too. My job as their leader was to let them.

Gratitude in moments like this one are profoundly important. You can't complete a project like the rebuild of the hotel without a community of people who show up when you need them most.

When you're trying to build a life doing new and big things, it is the little things you share during the struggle that make it possible to keep pushing, to persevere.

Except I think most people get gratitude wrong. They are grateful after the fact. They are grateful within the privacy of their own thoughts. Their gratitude appears in contemplation and reflection, when the work is over and the deeds have been done and they have the benefit of knowing, by virtue simply of being alive, that they've weathered the worst of it. At least for the day. To me that doesn't feel like gratitude, it feels like relief.

I'm grateful for my family . . . and that they are still healthy.

I'm grateful for my job . . . so that I can keep putting food on the table.

I'm grateful for my partner . . . because it means I'm not alone.

We focus our gratitude wrongly on the positive, too—grateful for the bullets dodged, what didn't go wrong. As though we can pick and choose. Nietzsche said we were free when we stopped simply bearing what life sent our way and started to love it. True gratitude is incompatible with selectiveness. It's all-encompassing.

The fire. The floods. The betrayals. The breakups. The stress. The stupidity.

When you can tell me you love that, too, that you're glad it arrived at your door, then you are approaching gratitude.

It comes or goes for me, but like Burro Schmidt must have felt in those later years, I am sensing the breakthrough is coming.

The poet David Whyte says that gratitude "arises . . . from being awake in the presence of everything that lives within and without us," and from the understanding "that we are miraculously part of something, rather than nothing."

I know that feeling. Down in the mines, deep back in the farthest reaches of a tunnel, surrounded by darkness and silence and ghosts, is when I feel most connected to the mountain. It's when I feel most aware of everyone and everything that has ever been here or will ever be here. I feel at peace. Fulfilled. Certain that I've made the right decision devoting myself and my life to this place.

I'll confess, there are times when I'm alone with my thoughts at night before bed, when Cerro Gordo can sometimes feel like a gigantic con I'm running on myself. A delusion, like the one the big guy with the beard toted up here in his van, one of those projections we all try to stuff into the empty spaces in our lives.

And then, I see the faces of all of those who have sacrificed so much, who are willing to freeze their asses off on a frigid desert morning, to turn this dream into a reality, and I know that this is no con. These people weren't lured here by smooth talk and promises, they're here because they believe, deeply and at their core, in the same thing that I do, that what we're doing here is worth doing and worth doing well. They're here because they believe in building something that conserves the past and will last far longer into the future than any single one of us will. Perhaps this is too precious a thought, but sometimes I think that the Cerro Gordo that was, was built on darker human impulses, greed and vanity. But the Cerro Gordo that will be, will be built on a foundation of gratitude and humility. It will be a monument to the people who helped me build it.

And I am incredibly grateful to them and for them.

Still, gratitude isn't just about recognizing your good fortune. Nor is it simply about acknowledging it to yourself. It's also about showing appreciation for who or what has made that good fortune possible. I think to be truly grateful, or for gratitude to have impact on our lives, you have to feel it in the moment and you have to try to express it just as quickly. If the past is gone and the future isn't guaranteed, and the present is all we have, then now is the only chance you get to express gratitude.

When you're standing at the precipice of a major achievement, you need to stop and acknowledge verbally and directly the forces that have made this moment possible for you—whether that's God, or the wind, or a dozen strangers waiting for you 8,500 feet above sea level in the frigid purple light of dawn.

I've said that the old Cerro Gordo was built on a foundation of vice, and I stand by that. But that does not mean there were not those in town who understood gratitude and humility.

I've read many accounts in diaries and personal papers, mostly belonging to people who history would not count as winners of the Cerro Gordo sweepstakes, and there is always an appreciation for ol' Fat Hill who left the place behind. There's a tender melancholy in their words.

They all missed this place when it or they were gone. They may not have used the word, but it's gratitude that a lot of them are expressing—a humble thankfulness for having had the opportunity to spend time up here. But I could, of course, just be projecting.

The Cerro Gordo that was and the Cerro Gordo that will be binds you to it. Even when you don't accomplish your main goals for being there, enduring everything it can throw at you is an accomplishment all its own. It's a win. It's proof that you're made of sturdier stuff than maybe you thought. You've had your mettle tested . . . and it passed.

It's clear from the record that the men who first conquered this mountain—Beaudry, Belshaw, Gordon—expected, no, demanded, to be treated like gods. They had vision, to be sure, and grit. They accomplished what seemed impossible at the time. Were they proud of their achievements? Certainly. But they did not achieve what they achieved alone. The hands that turned their dreams to reality are the same hands that wrote those diary entries and journals long after they left Cerro Gordo. Were the men on whose behalf they toiled grateful? Perhaps.

Were they humble? I don't know. If they were, they left no record of it.

Then I think about someone like Chet Reynolds, who never came close to wealth by any objective measure. No one would ever claim Chet was a god. Just one of Cerro Gordo's many Sisyphuses who either ran out of rocks to push or time to quarry them. Was Chet grateful? It's hard to imagine gratitude co-existing with whatever mindset led him to abandon all his personal effects up here. But maybe. Maybe the mountain didn't fill his pockets, but it fulfilled him in ways that you can't tally on a bank statement or hold in a briefcase.

I would understand if that were the case. I don't plan on leaving this place with anything to my name or in my possession. I plan on leaving it all up here. In one hundred years, if someone were to stumble upon a duffel bag full of my things, I could absolutely imagine that person tallying up all those objects and coming to the conclusion that the story of the person who owned them might be a sad one. And they wouldn't be more wrong, because they couldn't account for the memories and the moments (like this one) that I took with me proudly, happily, gratefully into my next life.

CHAPTER 15

MAKING YOUR MARK

There's a cigarette—a Marlboro Red, of course—smoldering away between his forefinger and index finger, as his hand glides just above the ornate carvings in the soft red rock. He won't touch the stone, but he wants to get close enough to feel the energy, the human touch left here long ago. He wouldn't want to leave behind a trace of the oils in his dry skin, or do anything that might hasten the demise of these precious relics of some long-lost culture.

The ancient artists had sacrificed so much to leave these tokens all across the desert here, some ten thousand of them it's estimated, impressionistic pictographs of bighorn sheep and heroic depictions of their own people's celebrated hunters, punctuated by inscrutable swirls, formidable and yet delicate. They're shielded now by a thin coat of desert varnish, a semi-clear substance that oozes from the rock over thousands of years of storms, and forms a dull glaze over the art. Once, in the time before time was counted by our numbers here, archaeologists tell us, these pictographs and petroglyphs were brightly painted—ochre for red, gypsum for white, charcoal for black, all mixed with precious animal fat and painted with brushes made from animal hair. Every drop of paint, every hair in the brush was wrested from this harsh land at great personal cost. Whatever these ancient artists were trying to tell us was so important that they were willing to sacrifice food and medicine and warmth to create these paintings.

"They're prehistoric," Tip tells me. He hacks into his handkerchief, and I can see spots of blood when he does. It's the color of ochre. "It was so long ago they don't even have a name for the humans who made them."

He shouldn't be smoking.

His doctor had made that perfectly clear. Not in the final stages of lung cancer. Then again, maybe that's why he was smoking. He had just made a trip up to see the specialists, and they had given him the long-time-coming news. Maybe this cigarette and the one after it, and the one after that, until he didn't have the strength to draw another breath, was his way of staring death in the eye. I thought for a moment about those old Marlboro ads, that rugged cowboy with the Red dangling from his lips as he rides the range. That old cowboy died of lung cancer.

But when we conjure him, we don't conjure him on his deathbed, tubes and masks and painkillers. We see him on high on his horse. Every man makes his mark.

Maybe Tip is trying to make his, shrouded in blue smoke, hacking up the last of his lungs, showing me these ancient carvings that few others have seen or bothered to notice, sharing his last secrets.

"Nobody knows why they made them," he tells me. Nor is anyone sure when they were made, though some are thought to date back to the end of the last Ice Age, when nomadic hunters first arrived in North America sometime in the Paleoindian Period around 10,000 to 12,000 B.C.E.

Whatever their original meaning might have been is lost to time. But they mean something to Tip. He discovered these particular petroglyphs, and simply the knowledge where they are and that they are is one of the many things that gave meaning to Tip's life. And now he is sharing that knowledge with me. And I am sharing it with you.

Like most of the petroglyphs in this part of the country, these are hidden in brown rock canyons, difficult to reach. It's possible that the painters were marking these remote spots as hunting grounds or commemorating a particularly good kill. In those days, the ancient hunters would either herd bighorn sheep into these box canyons and kill them from on high, or drive them over the cliffside where women, gathered below, would administer the coup de grâce. A band could live a whole winter on the harvest from one good run.

Or maybe it's only the hard-to-reach ones that survived, the rest of the art destroyed by more modern man making his more selfish mark.

There are some who believe that the painters were not honoring themselves with the paintings but their prey, imagining that by sacrificing their most precious commodities, food and warmth and medicine, to etch the image of these creatures into the stone, they were granting these creatures immortality, and guaranteeing that the next harvest would also be bountiful. In that interpretation, it's not the painting but the act of painting that's sacramental. They were ritually participating in that ongoing act of creation, and of destruction. The ritual was what mattered.

The paintings that we find now are just an echo of that ritual, like the reverberation in a church right after the organ has finished.

Or maybe they were just telling a story. We are, all of us, the stories we tell about ourselves. We tell our stories in the fervent hope that someone will hear them, remember them, retell them, and in the retelling, we will be remembered. We were here. Once.

"My favorite ones are really hidden. By mile marker seven. Wish I could show you," Tip said. I thought I heard a trace of sadness in his voice, though to note it would have embarrassed him.

There was a finality to the way he said it. But also, a bit of hope. He no longer had it in him to gallivant around the entire desert to show me every petroglyph he had found. The doctors in Reno had made that clear to him, and he had accepted their verdict with a measure of grace and serenity that I don't think I could have mustered if I were in his shoes.

He was now in his last days, and he was spending them, with his doctors' blessings, at the old "Hart Camp," founded ninety-plus years ago by one of Cerro Gordo's previous owners, J. Percy Hart, the man behind a company that called itself Silver Spear. Hart had bought all the land around here in the 1930s for $12,000 at a tax sale and built a cabin about a mile outside of town, on a point from which he could see the whole of Owens Valley spreading out before him.

It was always one of Tip's favorite places around Cerro Gordo, removed from the bustle and tourists of the main town; it was a sanctuary, though Tip would never use a word like that to describe it. He had a more economical way of assessing such things. If you were going to die, there were worse places to do it.

I came to know of Hart through the journal of Frances Mikulecky, wife of Stanley Mikulecky, who worked as a diesel mechanic at Cerro Gordo from 1940 to 1942. To hear her tell it, Hart was a complicated, conflicted, but stubbornly optimistic man. According to her journal, he faced stiff financial hardships during his tenure at Cerro Gordo, but refused to give in. At one point, he had a chance to sell the whole headache for three-quarters of a million dollars, the equivalent of $16 million today, which would have given him a profit of 600 percent on his initial purchase. He refused. Even though, at the time, he didn't have enough money to pay all his workers. He spent every waking hour trying to raise money to continue funding his dream.

An article in the *Los Angeles Times* in February 1942 stated that "With the issuance a few days ago of a permit to finance resumption of operations in the old Cerro Gordo mine near Keeler, Inyo County, that notable property started another episode in the cycle which has been in progress periodically since its discovery by three Mexicans in 1865."

In the article, Hart proudly detailed the production on the last full mining year: "In 1929 it yielded 8,000,000 pounds of lead, 290,420 ounces of silver and 786 ounces of gold." At today's prices that would be over $15 million worth of minerals. But where Hart really hoped to make his mark was in mining for tungsten, a rare mineral used, among other things, to harden steel.

Remember, this was on the eve of World War II and tungsten was suddenly very much in demand. German metallurgists had developed a tungsten carbide that could be used in artillery shells with deadly results. A single tungsten carbide shell could slice right through the armor on Allied tanks, and in those early days of the war, everyone wanted to get their hands on as much tungsten as their government coffers could afford.

Hart vowed to ramp up production immediately. He was certain he would make his mark, and if he could make it on the broadside of a Wehrmacht tank, all the better.

But, alas, his dreams of cornering the tungsten market never panned out.

He struggled for funding for the first few years, eventually persuading Wilfred C. Rigg of Beverly Hills, an oilman, to invest in diamond-tip drill bits to tap all the old veins to hasten the search for new ones. They found little. After three years and $250,000, Silver Spear went belly-up and Hart went bankrupt. All that remains of his dream are the etchings in the rock done with diamond drill bits. Perhaps the ritual of riches itself was the point, and these gouges in the stone are all that's left behind.

Those and the cabin where Tip is living out his last days.

I see myself captured in those etchings in the stone. I feel a kinship with Hart. I understand how this town and its promise consumed him. It consumes me. I know what it feels like to risk everything to revive this snake-bitten old place.

Do I own the town or does the town own me? It's the question that hangs over me, that haunts me. It doesn't seem to haunt Tip, who has no illusions of legal ownership, but seems comfortably authoritative and wholly captured by this place. I'm not sure what the other owners before me felt, but it was probably somewhere in between us both.

It's the end of the day, and Tip and I are leaning back in a pair of weathered folding chairs at Hart's Camp, a Marlboro Red firmly between his yellowed fingers.

He was never much for small talk. But now he's running out of breath, and I know that every word is precious. So it means something to me when he uses one of the few breaths he has remaining to say, "Good to see the hotel coming back. Damn fine work."

"Thanks, it's been a battle," I respond, zoning out in my view over the mountains.

"It's your thumbprint," Tip replies, allowing the words to linger as we both stare at the final moments of sun slipping just a little too quickly behind Mt. Whitney.

"It's important this town has someone like you at the helm," Tip eventually continues, stubbing out his cigarette on the arm of the chair. It leaves a black smudge.

"Have you read *The Story of Inyo*?" he asks, referring to the most detailed history of the Owens Valley area, written by W. A. Chalfant, son of P. A. Chalfant, the founder of the *Inyo Register*, the main newspaper in the valley at the time. "I just reread the bit about William Hunter, from the Hunter cabin," he says. "You should read it."

Tip hands me his book, the binding long since worn out, with sections reinserted upside down and sometimes backward. "I marked it in a few places."

Of all the men who ever carved their names into the rocky history of Cerro Gordo, few have left a more lasting mark than William Hunter. The cabin where he lived bears his name. He built it just after he arrived in town and purchased the Belmont Mine. Before I knew the history of the Belmont, I camped in its shadow during a long overnight trek into Death Valley. I scavenged stones to build a shelter and a fire pit. His stones and my fire pit are still there, somewhere. The Belmont was a relatively small mine. It never produced much. But still, Hunter managed to parlay it into a lasting legacy here. It's not just the cabin that bears his name; a few miles farther out, there's the Hunter Ranch, which he established to run the two hundred mules he had acquired for the mine. Beyond that there's Hunter Mountain, which features one of the most treacherous dirt roads in all of Death Valley National Park. Many a traveler has mouthed Hunter's name and a string of muttered curses on their way to the summit.

Closer to home, there's the Belmont Loop, which is even more narrow and dangerous than the path up Hunter Mountain. If the devil had a halo, it would be the Belmont Loop. It encircles Cerro Gordo Peak and marks the exact path that Hunter took with his mule teams to deliver his ore to the smelters and to pack out supplies.

It's all in the pages that Tip has marked for me.

"You can keep it," he says as I take the book from him. We both know what he is really saying. But we both pretend that we don't.

A man is the sum of what he leaves behind. To build anything worthwhile takes hard work and time. William Hunter spent fifteen years in these hills before the mines closed and he moved down into the valley to become a rancher and grow hay. I've been here three.

There will come a day when I can look back and measure the mark I've made. I don't know if what I'm building now will last as long or make as much of a mark as William Hunter made. I know I'll never get rich, but that's not why I came here.

William Hunter didn't reap a fortune from this place the way Beaudry or Belshaw did. But fortunes are fleeting. Instead, Hunter built a life and a family and a legacy that his children proudly carried deep into the twentieth century. Having come west from Virginia in the aftermath of the Civil War, he embraced risk and adventure and was a better man for having done so. This place bears his brand and, even now, a hundred and fifty years after he first arrived, his legacy continues to inspire people and nourish their ambitions.

I spent that night wandering through the book Tip gave me, navigating my way through the chapters by the markings Tip had left for me. And now it's morning, time to carve a little deeper into the work that lies before us. The water crew is ready. They're outside the Belshaw, waiting for me to give the word to get started.

Tip is there. Dressed and eager, though his failing body won't let him work, nothing can stop him from being part of it. Today's task is to once again tap the stones with our technological staff and get the water flowing freely here again. That was high up on Tip's "bucket list" for this place.

He'll join us as we descend into the mine.

"What's it gonna hurt?" he asked, walking into the cage. There's no arguing danger with a man who can count the number of weeks he has left on one hand, without even removing the cigarette from between his fingers.

The ride down was quieter than usual. Tip was shivering, coughing hard, every hack shattering the tomb-like silence.

"I'm fine," he said to no one, to everyone, to himself, between coughing fits.

Our mission that day, we believed, was simply to prime the pump. After several days of speculating on the reasons why the water had stopped flowing, we had settled on that as the likely problem. It was also possible that the intake for the pump had been set too high and that we had drained the water source just enough so that the pump was sucking air. There was also a chance that the pump had just given up the ghost completely, though we shuddered to contemplate that possibility.

Whatever it was, we wouldn't know for sure until we got down there and saw for ourselves.

When we hit the 700-level we were greeted by a large American flag strung across the mine shaft directly across from the hoist. We had left it there a year earlier to mark our last great achievement in the war for water here. We had all signed it when we first got the water flowing and left it there as a mark of our success. Even Tip signed it. I'm sure, a hundred years from now, some intrepid spelunker will descend into this mine, spot what remains of that flag on the wall, and wonder what the hell it's doing there. To them, that flag will be as inscrutable as the swirls on the walls of Tip's canyon.

And now we're at the 700-level. We all have our tasks. Craig's is to check the pump for any mechanical malfunctions. Tip and I will inspect the water source and examine the line for any noticeable issues.

"Lost its prime. We gotta move these rocks. Get the line down," Tip said, looking at the pile of rocks halfway to the ceiling of the shaft.

He was right. The eighty feet of tubing going from the water source to the pump had too big of an incline in it. Pumps don't like to draw water up from the water source.

Back at the pump, Craig was going through all the wiring and adjusting it to draw less water per hour.

That left Tip and me to move dust-covered rocks, some ten pounds, some fifty pounds, all of them sharp from fracture, to make a path for the water line. Tip's breath came ragged. The spots of blood he hacked up were thicker, redder now.

"I got it, Tip," I said, moving the rocks as quickly I could, hoping if I moved fast enough there'd be nothing left for him to do. He would have none of it. Even though he was convulsed by racking coughs, he got down on his hands and knees, and painfully tossed heavy stones aside. His knees left a trail in the dust and slag, an imprint in the earth that would remain long after our work was done.

I didn't have the heart to stop him. Even in his last days, Tip was giving everything he had to Cerro Gordo. Who was I to tell him no?

It took far longer than it should have for Tip to finally slow his pace. But eventually the weight of the stones, the silica dust, and the crushing weight of his own mortality proved to be too much for this tough old truck driver. He rested.

Soon enough, we were done. We all made our way to the water source to admire our own handiwork. That's when we caught sight of it. There, right above the water line, etched by hand in burned carbide on dusty rock, was a name.

"Roy."

We'd seen such markings before. Somewhere in almost every adit in the Union Mine some old-time miner had left his name on the rock. Most of them had signed their names at several locations. But this was the first time any of us had seen Roy's name.

We knew nothing about him, nothing at all, except that once, at least, he had made it down this deep into the mine, and had stood where we were standing, and perhaps done something similar to what we had just done. That's all we needed to know about him. That whoever he was, he was one of us.

"Roy must have been a hell of a man," Tip said softly.

A hell of a man indeed.

There have been other men down there. Men like us. There was

Juan, who paired his name with a rude drawing of a duck, and Karl, who also wrote "Cerro Gordo Mines" in surprisingly elegant cursive. There was George, who helpfully noted that he was from Bakersfield, to distinguish himself from all the Georges in Cerro Gordo.

Ethnographers have a word for this kind of thing. They call it "symbolic immortality," and it's done the world over, and has been since the beginning of time. Graffiti has been found in ancient ruins in Europe and the Middle East. During World War II, when tungsten shells were tearing through Allied and German tanks all over Europe, one or more anonymous GIs decorated war-ravaged buildings and the burned-out wreckage of halftracks left in the wake of the most savage battles with the cheerful image of a man with a large nose peering over a wall, and the phrase "Kilroy was here."

No one knows who Kilroy was, or whether he survived the war. But Kilroy is immortal all the same.

So are Roy and Juan and George from Bakersfield. And so is Tip.

Each of them faced hardship, each of them made some sacrifice, and each of them left their mark. For Tip, his mark is in the painful tracks he left in the dust at the bottom of the mine, and in the secret knowledge he etched in my mind about the ancient petroglyphs.

The very act of making the mark is an act of creation, a ritual, a defiant fuck-you to the tyranny of time. The mark itself is just an echo, the sound a stone makes when you drop it nine hundred feet into the mouth of a mine.

It was time to go. Tip lingered outside the cage a bit longer than usual. The water was pumping now, and the pipes thudded and clanged. He seemed to be drinking in the sound.

And then, abruptly, he said, "All right, let's go."

The next time I ventured out to hunt for petroglyphs, Tip was too

Air

weak to join me. And, so, I took Tim Australia into the blazing desert sun. But Tip was still with us, in a way. We followed the trail he had blazed, navigated by the odd landmarks that had caught his eye when he first wandered here.

"Take a left at the old barrel." "When you see the rock that looks like a heart, turn right." The desert is still, but it's not a still life. Rocks shift, barrels roll, and there were a few times when Tip's description of the landmarks lasted longer than the landmarks themselves. There were a few dead ends, places where Tip's prescribed path ended up in some sandy draw with nothing to distinguish it from any other nowhere in the desert. But Tim, a crafty man, had managed to suss out all of Tip's directions with enough usable information that he was able to create a map and save it on his GPS device.

We set out on our dirt bikes. It was a brutally hot August day; the heat was almost too intense for our engines. We left a trail of coolant in the sand wherever we went. Eventually, we found a spot in the desert where Tip and Tim's map both agreed there would be petroglyphs nearby.

We left our helmets dangling from the handlebars and began our hike in the vague direction of "canyons." There are lots of canyons out there.

We didn't talk much along the way. Tim is not the sort of man who is eager to indulge in philosophical discourse; it's a waste of good spit when the sun's this hot. I tried. I wondered aloud why the ancient artists had chosen the particular images they had, the sheep, the hunters.

"I dunno, why do fuckwits carve their names in everything around here? To be remembered."

It was as good an answer as I was going to get. It was as good an answer as any.

Every person wants to be remembered. Every person wants to leave something behind that says, "I was here; I did my best." Everyone who ever had a hand in building Cerro Gordo wanted to be remembered forever. Every person who is rebuilding this old mining camp deserves to be remembered.

But it's not enough to be remembered. You—me—all of us, have a sacred obligation to remember all those who came before us, all of those who are with us now. Memory is a sacred trust. Remembering is an act of creation, of resurrection and renewal. It's a ritual and a sacrament and promise, a pledge we make that binds us to the past and the future. And by connecting to that something larger, your life will be that much more rich.

Tip never said any such thing to me. But I learned it from him all the same. And I make this pledge to him now.

I will remember. Tip Earl Shields.

CHAPTER 16

MAKE A JOYFUL NOISE

It's the most lonesome sound there is, a steel spade cutting into the scree to hollow out a grave. Even a small one.

I listened as John Bowden dug it out. Near the top of the hill in the old cemetery not five yards from the ancient pinyon pine that he and I used to sit under on a hot afternoon. Tip hadn't asked for much, just a small hole up here to hold his ashes. You'd think that would have been easy to do, a small task when you consider all the shovels full of earth that have been turned up here over the years. Truth is, I don't think I've ever seen a heavier clod of earth lifted.

Dust to dust.

Tip's send-off was small, just a few of us. Bowden, Tip's old part-ner who had explored every inch of the valley with Tip over thirty years, had brushed off his good black Stetson for the funeral. I had pulled on my best dress boots. Craig was there, so were Cody and

Dave. John Miller of Miller's Towing, the man who had lent us his Bobcat, the same Bobcat that Tip had patiently trained me to use, made an appearance. Sean Patterson, the man who had owned this town before me, and is still, in a way, owned by it, was there. A couple of rockhounds whom Tip taken under his wing rounded out the tiny clutch of mourners.

None of us were much for prayer. There were no homilies. But in our minds, we beat the drum slowly, played the fife lowly, and we laid the sod o'er him, down in the green valley.

It takes a cold man to stand beside the grave of a friend and not at least think about the eternal.

I found myself thinking about those old desert wanderers and their book. If you believe their version of the beginning, everything that ever was and ever will be was willed into existence from nothing. The light and the darkness, the heavens and the earth were conjured out of the void; so were the birds of the air, the fish of the sea, and every creature that walks or crawls or slithers on the land, all of them came from nothing. All except one. When their god made man, they tell us, he scooped up a handful of earth and breathed life into it. You can believe their story or not.

But even if it's just a fable, there's a truth in it, an acknowledgment that we are not just another creature in this world, but that the world is in us, part of us, flesh of our flesh and bone of our bone.

Tip loved this place, and if you take a rest on the small bench just behind his grave, you can look out and see all the places that mattered to him, the places where Tip left his mark. You can see the hoist house where our frantic search for water began. You can see the bunkhouse, the first project he laid his hands on when he came into town. And you can see his last project. It's an outhouse.

Ashes to ashes, dust to dust, remember, man, that thou art dust, and unto dust thou shalt return.

I used to think that incantation was an admonishment, a warning from a bunch of white bearded patriarchs to their unwashed flock not to get too uppity. You're nothing.

I realize now that I was wrong. It's not an admonishment, it's an exhortation. You are the land and the land is you. You are everything.

This land got deep inside of Tip, and Dave and Craig and Cody and Bowden and Sean and Miller and the rockhounds and me. It is part of all of us, and now Tip is part of that land.

John tamped down the last shovel load of dirt and rocks on Tip's grave and we all took turns telling our favorite stories about Tip. It seemed he had taken each person there under his wing in some way. Quietly guiding them at different stations of their life. For a man who had a reputation of not having many friends, he certainly impacted those in attendance deeply. Deep, not wide.

The way Tip enjoyed studying as well.

We wandered down to the museum deck where I had prepared some chairs and drinks. It was only about noon when the libations ran dry, and the last of the gathering filed out. It was still far too early for my sunset pilgrimage to my special rock, but that day, the mountain was calling and I knew I must go.

And so, a bit slower than I normally would, I tossed a leg over my dirt bike, kicked her conscious, and roared off. I sped past that outhouse, its ridiculous, multi-hued paint shimmering in the midday sun. I remember arguing with Tip over that. I wanted to paint the damn thing brown, the color an outhouse ought to be, but Tip had been adamant, all the colors of all the stray pieces of wood, salvaged from somewhere else, would remain. I relented. I'm glad I did. I don't think an outhouse ever made me smile before.

Beyond that was the bunkhouse. Tip's first project. It had been a solitary labor of love for him. He preferred to work on it alone when he first arrived here; he hadn't yet found his place in the community, was still working on the whole plays-well-with-others thing, and this dilapidated ruin was as good a place as any to stake his claim. He sweated and groaned, he ripped out the rabbit brush that was swallowing the place with a truck and a strong chain and, bit by bit, he willed the place back to life.

I can smell the sweet mesquite smoke rising from a grill on the porch of the bunkhouse as I roar by. A half dozen volunteers are making lunch. Not a single one of them knows that they've got a roof over their heads thanks to Tip's backbreaking efforts. That would have pleased him. It pleases me.

A bit farther on, I catch sight of the hoist. Seven hundred feet below it, the pump is humming. Water from the rock. I'm sure that makes Tip happy, wherever he is.

I pass Hart's Camp. Tip's ragged old armchair is still there, right where it was when he and I last spoke, the ash mark from his cigarette still visible, I'm sure.

That very last talk, Tip had given me marching orders. There were three things he said that I ought to do. "Ought to" was as close to a direct order as Tip ever gave.

The first was to find all the petroglyphs. That was already on my list. The second was to hike to a town called Beverage, and third was to walk a difficult and challenging wash beyond Hart's Camp.

I knew the place, from a distance anyway. I could see it twice a day, every day, from my sunrise and sunset rock. But I never thought to actually walk it. It was too steep, too many cliffs.

Tip assured me that it was worth the risk.

I trusted Tip on such matters. I still trust him. I could not think of a better day to let him guide me down that ragged wash. And so, I hopped off my bike and set off down the wash.

I was utterly unprepared for the demanding hike. I was still wearing my good dress boots from the funeral, with their citified smooth soles, fine for line dancing, maybe, but useless on this shale. The second I hit the trail, I started sliding sideways on the loose gravel, muttering curses at my boots. Tip would have gotten a kick out of that. Probably would have laughed out loud.

That made me chuckle.

A few yards down, and I looked up at the remains of Hart's Silver Spear mine. Hart's dream had crumbled there, and it was still buried under a pile of rotting wood and rusting corrugated steel from what must have been a roof.

Tip had found something out here that he wanted me to see. He never said exactly what it was, and so I pushed on. The deeper I went, the more relics I stumbled across, rusted fragments of old ore buckets, slowly turning to sand, ancient planks petrifying, century-old oil cans being buried by the wind and the rain. In time, there'd be no trace of these things, at least none that you could see with the naked eye. But they wouldn't be gone. They'd be part of the mountain.

I followed the trail until I hit a dead end, a forty-foot cliff. Even if I hadn't been wearing ridiculous shoes, that cliff would have stopped me in my tracks the same way my progress had been stalled on the Salt Tram trail. I'm sure Tip had a few choice words for that damned cliff when he ran into it. I could hear him snickering over my shoulder as I scrambled back up the steep, sharp shale, over a small ridge, and down into an alternate wash to continue the trek.

"Just walk the wash," he had told me more than once. You never know what you might find.

Yeah, sure, Tip.

Farther down.

An old shoe, mummified by the relentless sun. A broken beer bottle. Tip and I had found one just like it on our first hike together.

A sardine can. I remembered how excited these old cans made him. Monuments in stone of generals on horseback in big city parks are all lies, fantasies of a past that never was. A crumbled tin, a relic of a miner's lunch, that's a real memorial to the past. Every one of them is a treasure.

From here, I could see all of Death Valley. The wash extended downward, cut back toward the back road into Cerro Gordo and down past the Ella Mine, the first mine I ever explored with Tip.

"Where are you taking me, Tip?"

"Just walk the wash. If you're ever in need of an adventure, just walk the wash."

The heat was starting to hit me; I was starting to feel the first throbbing signs of dehydration, just as I had on the snake-bit trek to the Salt Tram. But I kept going.

I slipped and stumbled around a turn in the wash, and then I saw it.

At first, I thought it was a mirage. My sunbaked brain playing tricks on me. Serious botanists had assured me that such a thing was not possible here. But there it was, right in front of me, growing in the unforgiving rocks, a lone bristlecone pine, stout and gnarled, a hunchback ogre of a tree, defiantly clinging to the shale, shaking its fist at the sky as if to say, "I'm alive in a place where the experts told you no life can exist."

In the midst of life we are in death.

In the midst of death we are also in life.

That's one of the things I notice whenever I look closely, like Tip taught me. What seemed like inhospitable, empty, abandoned land, suddenly reveals its secrets. Footprints are everywhere.

You realize you're not alone. You realize that there are some survivors around you, biding their time, thriving off the land.

There's another such tree up the road an hour or so. They call it Methuselah, after the most ancient of the ancient desert wanderers, because it is believed to be among the oldest living things on earth. I've visited with Methuselah many times. It was a seedling when the ancient Britons hauled their boulders to Stonehenge. It outlived the pharaohs who built their monuments to themselves at Giza, and it was already ancient when the first stone was laid for the Great Wall of China. The winds that rustled through his branches blew around the globe and rustled the hem of Aristotle's garment, and Alexander's, and Jesus's. Methuselah is the oldest living organism on Earth, estimated to be around five thousand years old.

This rugged bristlecone pine that Tip had led me to is not as old as Methuselah. But the fact that it's here at all is a kind of miracle. This patch of sand and shale should never have been able to give it succor. And when, by some fluke, it did take root, its survival was always threatened. It was already here, when the miners first came. Those men would have swung an ax at anything if they thought they could get a yard of timber or enough firewood out of it to allow them to shiver through a desert night. Three dead stumps beside it are proof enough of that. How did this misshapen survivor escape their covetousness?

And yet escape it did, and it did it by standing right where it is, and right where it will be, perhaps for millennia.

There is a profound beauty in this squat, gnarled tree, a kind of rugged grace in its twisting, many-armed trunk that rises up like some ossified sea creature, an octopus in the desert, a regalness in the sparse laurels of green leaves it wears like a crown. It broods, this tree. It conserves its energy. It has, I imagine, grown less than an inch in the century and a half since Belshaw arrived in Cerro Gordo. A hundred years after my death, it'll stand an inch taller still.

But stand it will.

This is what Tip wanted me to find.

It's funny, sitting on those rotted old chairs at Hart's Camp, Tip and I had talked often about bristlecone pines, about their sheer stubbornness, their too-tough-to-dieness, and their rarity.

They grow, but they do it alone, and they do it in secret places. Never once did he mention that he'd discovered this one.

I think I know why. I think he wanted me to discover it for myself.

That's what a teacher does, that's what teachers have done ever since the breeze that blew through Methuselah's branches rustled through Zeno's beard as he lectured at the Stoa Poikile. They don't tell you what to think, or see; they teach how to search.

I sit on one of the stumps and I'm close enough to touch the bark of Tip's bristlecone. Touching the tree fills me with peace. A few of its cones have fallen into the wash. A few winged seeds are still attached to them. I pick up one of the cones and roll it around in my hand. One of the seeds falls free and I place it my pocket. A souvenir, a talisman.

When I get back to town, I wander over toward the hotel. There used to be an old pine just outside the front door. The night of the fire, when it was clear that the hotel was lost, one lone firefighter turned his attention toward saving that tree. He doused it with water. But it was too late. The flames had already charred half of its trunk and singed most of its branches. It clung to life for a few weeks, but eventually the old tree gave up the ghost.

The hotel itself is now returning to life. Inside, the walls are now up. The old timers were right, framing goes up much faster than concrete goes down. You can feel the vitality returning to the place. I take great joy in that.

Still, it seems to me that something's missing. It needs a tree to cast its loving shade on the porch on a hot summer's afternoon. I go back to my cabin, grab my spade and return, pacing off twenty feet from the card room window. I reach into my pocket and place the seed from Tip's bristlecone gently in the ground. There's nothing like the sound of a spade cutting into the earth to plant a tree. It makes a joyful noise.

EPILOGUE

Walking into the hotel now I can feel the spirit returning to the area. Every empty corner filled.

Soon this entrance will welcome guests from all over the world. Mining enthusiasts who want to stay where Mr. Belshaw once did. Europeans, fascinated with everything Death Valley. Rockhounds searching for that one piece of smithsonite to complement their collection. Desert rats, stopping through on a motorcycle ride deeper into the valley. Fans of Ghost Town Living, who have been following along for years, watching every board on this hotel be laid. They'll all come, as guests have been coming to this doorway for the last century and a half. There will come a day when this new wood will be worn down by the boots of visitors the same way the old wood was. I long for that day.

I step into the barroom and run my hand along the bar. It, too, is worn smooth over time.

One of the old owners used to be famous far and wide around here for his ability to sling a frosty mug of root beer all the way down that bar, and I feel it incumbent on me to do the same. I've been practicing, and I've developed a solid twenty-foot slide with practically no English on it all.

I like to imagine myself sitting at the bar for many years to come, getting old here, meeting new friends who have answered the call of this place, sliding them a beer.

I'm starting to dream about the grand opening party.

We could pack this place a hundred times over with the people who have helped. I'm not much of a piano player but I've been practicing the Chopin that Doc Holliday played in the movie *Tombstone*. I hope I can play it by the time the first night rolls around.

The sound of engines idling outside the window rouses me from my reverie. Yellow Jeeps, a group of tourists of some sort in red jackets, mingling in the parking lot. They seem to be pretty excited to be here. I know that feeling—it's the same feeling I got the first time I saw this place.

It's the feeling you get on your first visit that brings you back for your second, and for a certain number of them, it'll keep them coming back until one day they just decide that they belong here and they're never going to leave. I play a little game with myself, scanning the tourists, trying to see if I can tell which ones will fall hopelessly in love with this place. It's a fool's game. If somebody sized me up that way when I first came here, I doubt that anybody would have picked me for a future lifer at Cerro Gordo.

That's the thing. Cerro Gordo takes you as you are, but then it changes you. It changed me. I'm sure it will change some of them.

Sure, some of them will see their trip up here as a brief and pleasant diversion. And that's fine.

But others, maybe only a few, will come away from this trip thinking, "This place is important, this place matters, this is a place where I could belong."

Beyond the group's red jackets there's another group led by Abby, our resident tour guide.

They're over by the theater. The wind carries her voice as she explains the history of the building. "Originally a mechanic's garage in 1904 . . ." Her facts are wrong. But hell, she's a volunteer and her group is enjoying her spiel. We can correct the record later. Right now, let them all enjoy the moment.

It's been almost four years. I came up here with hopes of bringing a dead town back to life. Cerro Gordo has returned the favor in spades. It no longer feels like a ghost town, though there are ghosts who dwell here, or at least they dwell in me. It feels alive and vital. And so do I.

I try not to measure myself against those men who came here before me. But I can't help it. I wonder what Simpson would think of this new hotel. I wonder what Belshaw would think of what we've done here. Or Gordon. Or Tip.

There's an ornate box sitting beside what will soon be the front desk of the American Hotel. In it is a gift somebody sent me, a beautiful sundial, and etched around its perimeter is the phrase "Each hour cuts, the final one kills."

Tempus fugit, memento vivere. Time flies, remember to live.

Every moment of every day is precious, and every moment you don't spend living, really living, is a moment you spend dying. Life is action. We are what we do.

So do more. Start the crazy project. Dig out your inner Burro Schmidt and start swinging.

Do, as if your life depended on it. Because it does. Find something to give your life to and give your life to it. Do not go to the grave with a song still in you. Doing so not only hurts you, it hurts future generations looking for people like Burro Schmidt to inspire them on their own journeys. People are drawn to those giving their all, even if they don't understand why. You know, and that's good enough.

It's a cliche, of course, that so many people are filled with regret on their deathbeds. They say, "I wish . . .", "I wish . . .", "I wish . . ."—a catalog of things they had hoped to do but now cannot. When it's time for me to be added to the Cerro Gordo cemetery, I want to be able to say, "I'm glad . . .", "I did . . .", "I'm good . . ." And the surest way to make that happen is to never put anything off. To live, to work, to do, to be, today and every day after.

They've called this place a ghost town for a hundred years. I don't think we should call it that anymore. It's a word in the past tense. Haunted. Empty. Stalked by the spirits of the miners who struggled here and those who died, the hundreds in the cemetery, the forty somewhere at the bottom of a mine. It's a word with no present and no future. It's a word that does not apply to Cerro Gordo. Not now. Not in the future, if I have anything to say about it.

I'm casting about for another word to describe it, a word that captures all the contesting feelings that it evokes, the supreme joys, the crushing disappointments, the loneliness and the kinship and

camaraderie that I've felt here, the shame I've felt over my own ignorance and the exhilaration I've felt when I learned something new. A
word that embraces all the things I've lost and all the things I've
found. I need a word big enough to embrace all that and wide
enough to encircle all the people who feel the same way about this
place as I do.

I think I found it.

I'm not going to call Cerro Gordo a ghost town anymore.

I'm just going to call it home.

ACKNOWLEDGMENTS

I first want to thank the hundreds of volunteers who have made the trek up to Cerro Gordo in the past few years to help make a dream a reality. Whether it was mixing concrete on a freezing cold day, standing up a wall to an old cabin, or bringing up extra water to keep us all hydrated, Cerro Gordo would not be where it is today without all of your contributions. The sense of community you all created here means everything to me. Together, we've turned a town on the brink of being forgotten into a place that many more generations can enjoy. I hope you all feel a connection to the town and what we've done. I see the enjoyment it brings people every day and know it's thanks to you all.

Next, this book would not exist without the advice, mentorship, and friendship of Ryan Holiday. Over the past decade, I've been fortunate enough to sit in the front row as Ryan mastered his art, and it's always inspired me to do more. His advice on this book, this town, and more reminds me why millions turn to his writings today.

Thanks, too, to Nils Parker, whose conversations during the early stages of this book helped it become possible. And Byrd Leavell, agent extraordinaire, who believed in me, the idea, and the town, and brought this book to the world. Thank you to Seamus McGraw, who got me across the finish line when I stumbled. Your understanding of the desert and the struggles therein were unmatched.

My editor, Matthew Benjamin, was amazingly patient, supportive, and brilliant as this book came to life. Thank you for also believing in me, the book, and the twists and turns we had along the way.

Special thanks to Scotty and Richard who watched over Cerro Gordo during a historically bad winter so I could sneak off to Florida and work on this book for a month.

Also, thank you to Haley, who was there in Florida, the freezing winter, and all the ups and downs pulling this book together. You're the most creative person I know.

Thank you, too, to Aaron Saltzman, who not only originally sent the real estate listing for Cerro Gordo, but patiently sat through hours of rants about the tougher times here and still remained Cerro Gordo's biggest cheerleader. Thank you for your years of friendship and conversations. I'm excited to see where this journey we're on is going to take us over the next decade or so.

I owe a lot of my feeling of comfort and home at Cerro Gordo to the original "water crew" who helped get the water going again—Dave Mull, John Bowden, Tip Shields, Craig Leck, and Cody Royce. Thank you all for welcoming me and allowing me to feel like a part of the local community. Thanks, too, to Tim Australia, who was always down for whatever wacky adventure may be in store. I'm glad you found your way up here during that first snowstorm.

Finally, thank you to everyone who has watched this journey play out in real time on YouTube and elsewhere. In the middle of the pandemic, removed from everything, I found a community online. A support system that would carry me through some of the hardest times of my life. Every view, every comment, every email of support made this whole thing seem possible. So thank you all, so so much. I hope many of you get the chance to visit the town someday so I can thank you in person.

ABOUT THE AUTHOR

BRENT UNDERWOOD is the owner of Cerro Gordo, a mining town established in 1865. In addition to his work restoring the long-abandoned town, he's a partner at Brass Check and has worked with authors like Tim Ferriss, Tony Robbins, and Ryan Holiday. Brent currently lives on a mountain with no running water, seven cats, six goats, and at least one ghost.